The Satire of John Marston

The Satire of John Marston

A DISSERTATION

PRESENTED TO THE
FACULTY OF PRINCETON UNIVERSITY
IN CANDIDACY
FOR THE DEGREE OF
DOCTOR OF PHILOSOPHY

BY

MORSE S. ALLEN

HASKELL HOUSE
Publishers of Scholarly Books
NEW YORK
1965

published by

HASKELL HOUSE

Publishers of Scholarly Books

30 East 10th Street • New York, N. Y. 10003

Library of Congress Catalog Card Number: 65-26460

TABLE OF CONTENTS

APPENDICES

THE SATIRE OF JOHN MARSTON

BIOGRAPHY[1]

John Marston was born about 1575 and died June 25, 1634. He came of good family and was a gentleman. This was acknowledged even by his enemy, Jonson[2], who in fact lays stress upon Marston's own insistence upon his gentility. His family was an old Shropshire one; a Robertus de Marston is mentioned in 1307. The dramatist's great-grandfather was also a John Marston whose son Ralph was of Shropshire, while the next generation, John, the poet's father, was of Coventry.

The dramatist's mother, Mary Guarsi or Guersie, was probably the descendent of Balthazar Guarsi, a man of some prominence, living in the reign of Henry VIII[3]. Andrew Guarsi, Marston's grandfather, who died in 1561, was probably Balthazar's son. He bequeathed to his daughter Mary £100, to be paid when she should reach the age of eighteen, or upon her marriage. This Mary Marston, who was the poet's mother, died June 12, 1621.

John Marston, the poet's father, entered the Middle Temple in 1570. He seems to have moved to Coventry soon after, though he kept up his connections with London. In his will he calls himself "of city of Coventry Gent." In Dugdale's *Warwickshire* he is mentioned as a reader in the Middle

---

[1] The facts concerning Marston's biography are for the most part taken from the introd. to Bullen's ed. of Marston (which he summarized for the *D. N. B.*); and from Grosart's introd. to *Marston's Poems*, in his *Occasional Issues*. These *Issues* of Grosart are rare, only about fifty copies of each having been printed.

[2] *Poetaster*, II, i, 89f, and III, i, 27; 198. Cf. also infra, p. 63.

[3] He was an Italian, and surgeon to Queen Katharine of Aragon; he was naturalized in England in 1521-2; Bachelor of Medicine from Cambridge about 1530; and was surgeon to Henry VIII. In 1543 he was collecting for the king accusations against Archbishop Cranmer. By special grace he was admitted M. D. at Cambridge, 1546. Royal favor ended with the king's death, and we find him excepted out of the act of general pardon by Edward VI. However, he was made a Fellow of the College of Physicians in 1556. He was buried Jan. 10, 1557-8.

Temple in 1592, and there is preserved a letter of his to a mayor of Coventry, bearing the date October, 1597. He died toward the end of 1599. In the Temple records he is spoken of as "de Templo juris consultus in ecclesiae interiore Templi sepultus." His first two sons seem to have died when young; his third son was John. A fourth son, Thomas, married a Lucy of Charlecote. There were three daughters, Alice, Elizabeth and Margaret.

The dramatist, John Marston, was probably born in Coventry, though the records, incompletely preserved, do not mention his birth or baptism. Oldys, in his annotated Langbaine, says that Marston "died about sixty," which would place his birth about 1574. When he matriculated at Brazenose in February 1591/2 he was sixteen, indicating a birthdate of 1575 or 1576. Therefore his birth may with some degree of certainty be put down as 1575.

As was the case with Shakespeare at Stratford, Marston presumably attended the grammar school of his town. The Free School of Coventry had been endowed by John Hales in 1573, "with a learned master to teach grammar, a learned usher, and a man skilful in music to teach singing 'unto the children of all the free inhabitants within the city and inner liberties thereof gratis.' "[4] On "4 Feb. 1591/2, John Marston, aged 16, a gentleman's son, of Co. Warwick", was matriculated at Brazenose College, Oxford; he took his bachelor of arts degree on February 6, 1593/4, when only 18 years of age[5]. Wood says that "soon after completing that degree by determination[6] he went his way, and improved his learning in other faculties."

[4] Staunton's *Great Schools of England*, quoted by Grosart, Introd. p. x.

[5] Bliss's Wood's *Athen. O on.*, I, 762-3; *Fasti*, I, 602. Grosart shows Anthony à Wood to have mistaken for the poet a John Marston of Corpus Christi. Collier (*Shakespeare*, 1858, I, 179; *Bibliog. Account*, I, xxiv, note) mistook a John Marston, Preacher of S. Mary Magdalene, Cambridge, who was alive in 1642.

It is interesting to note that Robert Burton was in Brazenose after the long vacation of 1593, and so would have been acquainted with Marston.

[6] Determination signified an old examination given in the Lent following a candidate's presentation for a B. A. degree; it enabled him to proceed for an M. A., and seems to have been required. It was abolished early in the nineteenth century.

This probably signified that he studied law, as is indicated in a passage of his father's will:

"To s^d son John my furniture &c. in my chambers in the Middle Temple my law books &c. to my s^d son whom I hoped would have profited by them in the study of the law but man proposeth and God disposeth &c."

In fact the poet was buried in the Temple, and was registered there as "sometimes of the Middle Temple." In this connection Grosart mentions a passage in *What You Will*, I, i, 174:

> "We see the son of a divine
> Seldom proves preacher, or a lawyer's son
> Rarely a pleader; for they strive to run
> A various fortune from their ancestors."

Lawyers are seldom mentioned in Marston's satires, and at the end of his only censure of the law[7], he cautiously disclaims any intent to satirize "grave and reverent legists." This may have been because his father was still living. He contents himself for the most part with attacking the law's harsh terminology, the difficulties of which he himself probably experienced. It may be of his own attempts too that he speaks in the *Scourge of Villainy*[8], when he mentions

> "each odd puisne of the lawyer's inn,
> Each barmy-froth, that last day did begin
> To read his little, or his ne'er-a-whit."

> "Some span-new-come fry
> Of inns-o'-court."

In May, 1598, four years after Marston left Oxford, *Pygmalion and Certain Satires* was registered, and thereafter for a space of about eight years Marston must have been chiefly occupied with literature. The *Scourge of Villainy* was published later in the same year. On June 4, 1599, his *Pygmalion* and *Scourge of Villainy* were ordered burned for immorality, but this probably only increased their popularity.

[7] *S. V.* VII, 92.
[8] *In Lect.* 7; 77.
Ovid, in Jonson's *Poetaster*, is in many respects like Marston, detesting the law, and preferring the writing of licentious verse.

7

He revised *Histriomastix* in 1599, and late in that year he wrote *Antonio and Mellida*. Its conclusion, *Antonio's Revenge,* appeared early in the next year, and later in 1600, *Jack Drum's Entertainment*. About February or March, 1601, appeared *What You Will*. In this year his literary quarrel with Jonson reached its height, with Jonson's *Poetaster* appearing about June, and Dekker's *Satiromastix,* inspired by Marston, two or three months later. The *Malcontent* belongs late in 1603; the *Dutch Courtezan* and the *Fawn* to 1604. Early in 1605 he was working upon *Eastward Ho* with Chapman and Jonson, and contributed commendatory verses to Jonson's *Sejanus*. *Sophonisba* was written in 1606. In this year he seems to have left London, at least temporarily: the title page of the second edition of the *Fawn* (1606) states it was issued "as corrected of many faults, which by reason of the author's absence, were let slip in the first edition" (also of 1606). Furthermore, in this second edition Marston says, "Reader, know I have perused this copy, to make some satisfaction for the first faulty impression; yet so urgent hath been my business that some errors have still passed." This "business," Grosart suggests, may have been his studies preparatory to entering the church. A Latin pageant celebrating the visit of the King of Denmark to James I in 1606 was probably the last of Marston's literary work that we possess[9].

When Marston took orders we do not know. He was presented to the good living of Christ Church in Hampshire, October 10, 1616, and he formally resigned it on September 13, 1631, presumably from ill-health.

The date of Marston's marriage is unknown. His wife was Mary, daughter of the Reverend William Wilkes, Chaplain to James I and rector of Barford St. Martin, Wilts[10]. That Marston married while he was still writing plays is made probable by Jonson's sarcasm to Drummond, that Marston wrote his father-in-law's sermons, and the latter wrote Marston's plays. So far as is known, Marston had no children.

[9] Attempted assignments of other work to Marston are dealt with by Bullen, I, liv f.; lix, note 1; III, 418.

[10] Grosart (introd. xxii) guesses that Marston was curate at Christ Church and assistant at Barford S. Martin. Barford is six miles west of Salisbury, and at least thirty from Christchurch.

In 1633 six of Marston's plays, oddly enough without the *Malcontent*, which is perhaps his best, were issued anonymously by William Sheares. In a dedicatory address the publisher speaks of Marston as being "now in his autumn and declining age" and "far distant from this place," *i. e.* London. However, his will was made the next year in Aldermanbury parish, London, June 17, 1634; Marston was so ill he could not sign it, but made a rough mark instead. The Temple Church burial registry has the entry:

"1634, June 26. Mr. John Marston, Minister, sometimes of the Middle Temple, who died in Aldermanbury Parish: buried below the communion table on the Middle Temple side."

Anthony à Wood in a reference to Marston's father-in-law Wilkes says of Marston[11]:

"Dying 25 June, 1634, he was buried by his father (sometimes a counsellor of the Middle Temple), in the church belonging to the Temple in the suburb of London, under the stone which hath written on it *Oblivioni Sacrum*."

So his dedication of his satires at the end of the *Scourge* is "To everlasting oblivion."

Thus we have a fairly complete outline of Marston's life, although the dates of his marriage and ordination are unknown. His life seems to show the same division of interest as his literary work; as he was both a licentious dramatist and a divine, so in what he wrote he always shows a conflict between the desire to depict lust in striking forms, and a bent towards corrective satire.

The picture mentioned in his wife's will has disappeared, and we know nothing of his personal appearance save what

[11] *Athen.* I, 762. Marston's will is to be found in Bullen, 1, xv. His widow's will is given in full by Grosart. It is interesting for its evidences of affection for her deceased husband; most of the legatees are his friends. She desires to be buried by her "dear husband", and bequeaths "my dear husband's picture . . . unto his ancient friend Master Henry Walley of Stationer's Hall." She mentions "a trunk full of books with lock and key, and a book of Martyrs not in the trunk," the latter being perhaps the only one of her husband's books she cared to keep out. To the famous Puritan minister Edward Calamy she left a small sum; he was an opponent of Bishop Hall, as Marston had been, and may well have been a friend of Marston's.

we can glean from Jonson's hits at Crispinus in the *Poetaster;* these do not amount to much more than that Marston had red hair and small legs, and probably wore a feather in his hat[12].

Concerning his personal characteristics we know nothing save that he won his wife's affection; he had literary quarrels with Hall and Jonson; the latter claimed he beat Marston and took his pistol from him, and in an epigram Jonson accused him of personal cowardice[13]. His seems to have been a complex character, at war with itself and with the world. Altogether, I believe that it may safely be deduced from his writings, and from what we know of his life, that he belongs to the contemporary type of Malcontent, which is best known in the figure of Jaques, in *As You Like It*[14].

My purpose in what follows is two-fold. First, I desire to trace the progress of Marston's quarrels with Hall and Jonson, in both cases endeavoring to clear up previous misconceptions. Second, I propose to analyze the contents of Marston's formal satires, and the satiric elements in his plays, thereby contributing something to our conception of Marston and the satiric element in Elizabethan drama.

[12] Cf. infra, p. 56.
[13] Quoted infra, p. 74.
[14] For treatment of the Malcontent type, see infra, p. 143f.

THE QUARREL WITH HALL.

Marston's first literary work, his Satires, shows him already engaged in wrangling[1]. Joseph Hall, later bishop of Exeter and Norwich, was the object of his attack. At the time Hall was a young man about a year older than Marston himself, who was only twenty-three. Hall, who had been a fellow of Emmanuel College, Cambridge, began his extremely voluminous literary work with the publication of satires, *Virgidemiarum*, in 1597 and 1598, and won thereby a considerable reputation. Undoubtedly it was their favorable reception that inspired Marston, representing the other university, to publish satires also. He would be the more urged thereto, since he disagreed with some of the judgments pronounced by Hall.

Hall claimed to be the first Englishman to enter the field of satire. In the Prologue to Lib. I of the *Virgidemiarum* he says:

> "I first adventure: follow me who list,
> And be the second English satirist."

This claim cannot be substantiated; Hake and Lodge had already published poems calling themselves satires, and conforming to the type in almost every way[2]. But Hall was

[1] See Appendix A, for details of Marston's satiric references to Hall.

[2] Lodge had already asserted priority for himself. For this and other English satires before Hall, see infra, p. 85f. Hall was proud of being an innovator — he claims to be the first to write, in English, (besides Satires), Characters, Epistles and Aphorisms. Thus, in his 1608 dedication of his *Epistles,* to Prince Henry, he says: "Further, which these times account not the least praise, your grace shall herein perceive a new fashion of discourse, by Epistles: new to our language, usual to others." Ascham and Howell are usually said to have anticipated him with Epistles; for earlier writers of Characters, see Baskerville, *English Elements in Jonson's Early Comedies,* p. 68f.

Prof. H. V. Routh, *Camb. Hist. Eng. Lit.* IV, 377, gives Hall credit for priority in satire, since, as Grosart conjectures (*Occas. Issues,* IX, 1879; — *Bp. Hall's Complete Poems,* Memorial Introd., pp. vi-viii) Hall may have written his as early as 1591; and because Hall was first to

11

probably sincere in believing in his claim, since he shows no influence from any of the preceding English satires; and he adds in his Postscript to the Reader, that, save Ariosto "and one base french Satyre, I could never attaine the view of any for my direction." It must have been the case that Marston too knew of no other previous satires, else he would surely have refuted the false claims of Hall. But he seems to have been content to put himself into the second place Hall assigned to a successor.

The principal, perhaps the only occasion of Marston's attack upon Hall was, I believe, Marston's disagreement with certain critical literary opinions of Hall's.

Marston so far as we know had published nothing at the time of the publication of *Virgidemiarum;* and there are no evidences of any prior personal quarrel. I am sure there are no allusions to Marston in Hall's satires[3]. The only passage admitting of any real doubt is in Hall's last satire, which is supposed by some to have been added after the rest as a reply to Marston's attacks. The dates are clearly against this supposition[4]. The satire in question was entered in the Stationers' Register before any of Marston's work, and it is unlikely that Hall in print would have attacked work of Marston which was still in manuscript. Furthermore, the internal evidence is almost as conclusive[5].

adopt the tone of Juvenal, which became the prevailing one in English satire. The latter reason seems hardly sufficient for ignoring earlier satires; and in 1591 Hall would have been only seventeen years old; there is no evidence for so early a date.

[3] Cf. Schulze, who has done the most work on Hall's satires: *Die Satiren Halls,* p. 277; Grosart, *Occas. Issues,* Introd. to *Poems of Hall; Alden, Rise of Formal Satire in England,* pp. 141, 5; *C. H. E. L.,* IV, 380, where Routh disagrees.

[4] The Last Three Books of *Virg.* were entered March 30, 1598; Marston's first entry (*Pyg. and Certain Satires*) on May 27, 1598. Since Hall's last satire, the one in question, takes up the whole of his Sixth Book, it must have been included in the entry.

[5] The persons Hall attacks in Lib. VI, i, are called Labeo and Balbus. Most of the satire on these characters refers to Nash, as Schulze shows (p. 271f). Balbus had written for a long time (ll. 162-173); Marston had published nothing. Labeo is accused (ll. 186-190) of being an extremely slow and what Jonson called 'costive' poet, which does not sound like Marston. The passage (ll. 174-184) which Grosart says refers to Marston, and of which Alden says, "Certainly if any lines are to be so explained it should be these" (p. 145), is obscure. It

The title of Marston's satire against Hall (Sat. iv)[6]
Reactio, and its opening lines:

> "What cold Saturnian
> Can hold, and hear such vile detraction?"

seem to show Hall must have given the first offense. Had
Hall previously attacked Marston, we should have expected it
to be with reference to the poem *Pygmalion.* In the Satire
Reactio, written against Hall, Marston nowhere defends or
attempts to explain *Pygmalion;* but he does defend the work
of other poets whom Hall had attacked. Indeed, it might be
said to form Marston's Defense of Poesie. Thus, the address
to Hall at the conclusion of the satire reads:

> "Eat not thy dam, but laugh and sport with me
> At strangers' follies with a merry glee.
> Let's not malign our kin. Then, satirist,
> I do salute thee with an open fist."

(That Marston himself satirized some contemporary poetry,
was an inconsistency which would have troubled him not at
all.)

Besides the attack upon Hall's literary satire[7], *Reactio*
seizes upon the absurdities which Hall's vanity admitted into
the Defiance to Envy prefixed to the *Virgidemiarum.* Hall
in a patronizing way had professed to be a disciple of Spenser,
and had boasted grandiloquently that he could write various
kinds of poetry, "had he a mind to." To show how intricate
was Marston's parody, I quote some of his lines, prefixing
their number in *Reactio,* and suffixing the number of the
stanza of Hall's *Defiance of Envy* to which each refers:

is too long to quote; the best explanation I believe to be, that it is
meant by Hall to be a direct quotation put in Labeo's mouth, and
directed against Hall himself, "the controller of proud Nemesis."

Other passages have been vainly suggested, as I, ii, where it is asserted that Parnassus has been turned into a stews: here no particular
reference is meant; 1, ix, where a 'new laureate rhymed ribaldry and
recited acts of venery', refers to Nash (Schulze, p. 264-4) ; others are
I, ix, ll. 5, 8-9, 12; IV, iv, 14-15.

[6] The satires in *Pygmalion and Certain Satires* are here referred to
throughout by small Roman numerals; those of the *Scourge of Villainy (S. V.)* by capital Roman numerals. The division into books of
S. V. does not influence the numbering of the satires, which run con-
secutively.

[7] See infra, p. 162 (Appendix A).

13

131. "But come, fond braggart, crown thy brows with bay,   6
     Entrance thyself with thy sweet ecstasy   6
     Come, manumit thy plumy pinion,   7
     And scour the sword of elvish champion;   9
     Or else vouchsafe to breathe in wax-bound quill,   14
136. And deign our longing ears with music fill;......
139. Summon the nymphs and Dryades to bring   17
     Some rare invention, whilst thou dost sing   18
     So sweet that thou may'st shoulder from above   7
     The eagle from the stairs of friendly Jove   7
     And lead sad Pluto captive with thy song,   8
     Gracing thyself, that art obscured so long.   8
     Come, somewhat say (but hang me when 'tis done)   10
     Worthy of brass and hoary marble stone;   10
     Speak, ye attentive swains, that heard him never,   18
148. Shall not his pastorals endure forever?".......
151. Hath he not strongly justled from above   7
     The eagle from the stairs of friendly Jove?   7
153. May be, may be; tut! 'tis his modesty;.......
163. Envy, let pines of Ida rest alone,   1
     For they will grow spite of thy thunderstone;   1
     Strive not to nibble in their swelling grain."   1

This satire of Marston's is referred to by Edward Guilpin, in the sixth satire of *Skialetheia*, published in the same year as Marston's satires, 1598:

> "The double-volumed satire praised is
> And liked of diverse for his rods in piss;
> Yet other some who would her credit crack,
> Have clapp't *Reactio's* action on her back."[9]

[8] Bullen has the note (*Marston*, III, 286), "It is not improbable that Hall published an early volume of pastorals which is now unknown," and that in *Virg*. VI, i, 175-184, Hall replies to Marston's raillery. But Hall and Marston are expressly disclaiming the existence of any such pastorals. The latter part of Bullen's note is also incorrect (cf. supra.)

[9] Grosart (*Poems of Hall*, pp. xxv-vi) has been led astray in his interpretation of these lines, partly because of the confusion of the pronouns, and partly because "rods in piss" (i. e. in pickle), is found in Marston (*S. V*. i, 44; cf. J. D. E., quoted infra, p. 35) and not in Hall. But the phrase was not uncommon with the satirists of the time (cf. Weever, *Epigrams*, 1599, opening of the 'Intention') and has a classical source. In the second and fourth line of Guilpin, quoted above, *his* and *her* both stand for the modern *its*, and both refer to Hall's satires; *some* means Marston; *the double-volumed satire* is a reference to the two parts, *Toothless* and *Biting*, of *Virgidemiarum* of Hall.

Satire X, added in the second edition of the *Scourge of Villainy*, is dedicated by Marston "To his Very Friend, Master E. G.," who is supposed to be this Edward Guilpin. In this satire, Marston quotes what may be supposed to be Hall's answer to *Reactio:* "An Epigram which the Author *Virgidemiarum* caused to be pasted to the latter page of every *Pygmalion* that came to the Stationers of Cambridge." Doubt has been cast upon Hall's authorship of this epigram[10], but Marston's explicit statement throws the burden of proof on those who would deny it; and considering Hall's reasons for enmity and his Cambridge connection, there is little reason for ascribing it to anyone else[11].

Besides these two satires on Hall, references to him are scattered through Marston's satires[12]: Hall speaks so obscurely no one can understand him; he attacks little faults instead of great sins; Marston defends against him religious and other poetry, and attacks his style, frequently calling him "pedant", and ruder names. Most of this attack is unimportant and poorly done, and much is now hard to disentangle. Like almost all of Marston's satires, it is obviously the work of a young man, and not of much value.

So far the protagonists of this little literary mêlée have been traced; now come up the rascal rout of the reserves, in this case as usual anonymous or nearly so. A friend of Hall wrote a poem called *The Whipping of the Satyre,* which was entered in the Stationers' Register August 14, 1601. It was doubtless written soon after the appearance of the *Scourge of Villainy;* its publication had been delayed, perhaps, because of the ban of June 1, 1599, on satires. It is signed "W. I.", whom Nicholson has identified, from interior evidence, with a William Ingram of Cambridge. Quotations are here given at some length, because of the extreme rarity of *The Whip-*

[10] Alden, p. 145; Schulze, pp. 277-8.

[11] Might it not have been William Ingram who added the doggerel verses to Pygmalion? He was resident in Cambridge, and was Hall's friend in the quarrel (cf. infra). Marston might have honestly believed it to be Hall's. Of course there is no evidence of authorship save Marston's statement; and one would expect rather better verses from Hall.

[12] See Appendix A for a list of Marston's allusions to and borrowings from Hall.

ping, and because it speaks against Marston so tellingly[13]. The author begins by asserting that he

> "Dares scourge the Scourger of base villainy....
> What though the world was surfeited with sin,
> Must it of force his filthy physic lick?......
>
> Then know, thou filthy sweep-chimney of sin,
> The soil thereof defiles thy soul within.
>
> O wonder great! Is it not villainy
> That one should live by reckoning up of vice
> And be a sin-monger professedly
> In-voluming[13] offences for a price?
> Yet by the same doth purchase but the shame,
> And blaming others, merits others' blame.
>
> Thus you supposed the people's hearts to win
> By Machiavellian damned policy.
> For seeing men inclined to such sin,
> You feasted them with all variety,
> And lest you should this vilde pretence reveal,
> Did hypocrite it with a show of zeal.
>
> But hark, I hear the Cynic Satire cry,
> A man, a man, a kingdom for a man.[15]
> Why, was there not a man to serve his eye?
> No, all men turned to beasts that headlong ran.
> Who cried a man, a man then was he none,
> No, but a beast by his confession......
>
> He scourgeth villainies in young and old
> As boys scourge tops for sport on Lenten day;
> So scourgeth he the great town-top of sin,
> And puts his wit's felicity therein."

In a prefatory prose *Epistle* W. I. says, "Think you that foul words can beget fair manners? . . . You gathered up men's vices, as though

[13] The book has not been reprinted, though it was to have been in the *Isham Reprints*. Bullen quotes four stanzas. Collier has given an account of these Whipping books in his *Rarest Books,* IV, p. 235f., from which Alden gives some extracts. I quote from the fuller extracts given by Grosart, in his rare *Occasional Issues.*

[14] Orig., *Iouolumning.*

[15] The theme of *S. V.* VIII., A lyric Satire, beginning with the adaptation from *Rich. III.,* and repeating "a man, a man!" in lines 28, 46, 100. Cf. infra, p. 153, and E. H., III, iv, 5; W. Y. W., II, i, 125.

16

they had been strawberries, and picked away their virtues, as they had been the stalks.

They shall not make me believe, but that you were the Devil's intelligencer, for there went not a lie abroad, but it was presently entertained of your ear; and every sin kept under writing, for fear lest the devil, waxing almost six thousand years of age, should fail in his memory, and so chance to forget.

Beshrow my heart, if I do not think you a very prompt and politic gentleman: Prompt, wanting no words to express your anger; and politic, using much hypocrisy to conceal your malice. So that a man should blazon you aright, he must make you a tongue passant, your anger rampant, and your malice couchant."

Thus W. I. made the same criticism on Marston's satires, a year or two after they appeared, that almost all later critics have made[16]. Marston obviously took too much delight in portraying vice to make his punishment of it an effectual warning. Of course many of the things for which Marston is attacked in *The Whipping of the Satire* are equally true of Hall, the author's friend, or of any satirist. Satire presupposes more or less of a catalogue of sins[17].

A much poorer poem answered the *Whipping: The / Whipper of the / Satyre his pennance / in a white sheete: / Or, / The Beadles Confutation. / At London / Printed for Thomas Pauier / 1601.* It was entered November 6, 1601, obviously in rejoinder to *The Whipping*. I have not seen *The Whipper* save in extracts; Bullen calls it "the work of one of Marston's personal friends, or of some admirer who had more zeal than wit." Grosart[18] speaks of it as being nerveless, pointless and poor in every way. He says that it has been assumed to be Marston's own work, but has none

[16] Cf. infra, p. 117.

[17] Jonson, and, according to Collier, Nicholas Breton are pilloried with Marston in the poem, which is addressed "to the vain-glorious, the Satirist, Epigrammatist and Humourist." Humour plays and epigrams are meant in the following stanza:

"It seems your brother Satire, and ye twain,
Plotted three ways to put the devil down:
One should outrail him by invective vain:
One all to-flout him like a country clown;
And one in action on the stage outface,
And play upon him to his great disgrace."

[18] P. xix.

17

of Marston's characteristics, and contains the lines of encouragement, apparently from an outsider:

"Then friendly satirist, to thy pen again
Let not one private novice terrify
With halting lines, thy iron lasting brain,
Where sacred truth doth daily nutrify:
But with a brow according to thy heart,
Frown on the world, and give it his desart!"

After the rival factions have thus snarled at one another, there steps in a neutral as peacemaker, like the Prince to the Montagues and Capulets. Nicholas Breton is undoubtedly the author of *No Whippinge nor trippinge: but a kinde friendly Snippinge,* entered September 14, 1601. Though it has the air of closing the combat, from its date of entry it may have been written before the *Whipper.* Breton endeavors to make everybody happy, and gently discourages the writing of satires.

"It was my hap of late, passing through Paul's church-yard, to look upon certain pieces of poetry, where I found (that it grieves me to speak of) one writer so strangely inveigh against another, that many shallow wits stood and weighed against their follies."

The poem is a long one, and wanders far from its ostensible subject before the end; from certain references to plays of humours it is evident that it is in part a reproof of Jonson for ridiculing humours and gulls. Probably it also refers generally to the Stage-quarrel, at its height about this time; but its title places it with the Hall-Marston affair. Its references are so general, however, that its details are of little value[19].

Years after, Hall wrote a passage which seems to refer to Marston, then probably best known as the author of the *Malcontent.* One of Hall's *Characters, 1608,* was entitled *The Male-content;* it ends thus:

"He speaks nothing but Satyres, and libels, and lodgeth no guests in his heart but rebels. The inconstant and hee agree well in their felicity, which both place in change: but heerin they differ; the inconstant man affects that which will bee, the male-content commonly that which was. Finally, he is a querulous curre, whom no horse can passe by without barking at; yea, in the deep silence of night the very

[19] *No Whipping* has been republished in the *Isham Reprints.*

18

moone-shine openeth his clamorous mouth: he is the wheele of a well-couched fire-worke that flies out on all sides, not without scorching it selfe. Every eare was long ago wearie of him, and he is now almost wearie of himselfe. Give him but a little respite, and he will die alone; of no other death, than others welfare."

This quarrel between Hall and Marston, then, to judge from its literary remains was not very complicated. Marston was inspired to satire largely by the success of Hall, and perhaps partly by a desire to express disagreement with him. This is the only probable reason why Marston attacked the *Virgidemiarum.* Unfortunately it has never been a long step from critical disagreement to personal rancor. Hall himself made little (if any) reply, but Marston added a satire to the *Scourge,* ridiculing Hall. A friend of the latter, probably Ingram, attacked Marston in a verse pamphlet, and was poorly answered by an unknown supporter of Marston. About the same time Breton tried to smooth things over. There is no evidence in Hall's later writings that he himself carried on the direct quarrel, and I have discovered no references to it save the indirect one just quoted.

So far as we can judge, the quarrel was of no value to Marston, and did not redound to his credit; Hall by his very imperturbability, as well as by the real merit of his work, gained the victory, if a decision were to be made.

So far as Marston himself was concerned, the incident had ended before the much more important quarrel with Jonson began; but the way in which it was carried on is good evidence that Marston was ready for trouble. We know little about the grounds of the stage-quarrel; Marston's relation with Hall, however, would tend to make us believe that the later quarrel was not entirely Jonson's fault, since it is evident that Marston was not at all averse to entering the literary lists, and in the role of challenger.

19

MARSTON'S PART IN THE STAGE-QUARREL

The so-called War of the Theatres, or Stage-quarrel, created much excitement in the years about 1600, and has been the subject of much critical excitement since. I propose to discuss it here from the standpoint of Marston. He, with Ben Jonson, took the most important parts; Dekker was merely an auxiliary. The quarrel first came to light obscurely in certain dramas; there ensued an interchange of attacks in alternate plays of Marston and Jonson, each play growing more personal and less good-natured; finally the affair culminated in the open and bitter assault of the *Poetaster* and the reply, *Satiromastix*.

Eagerly-searching critics have of late drawn nearly a score of plays into the maelstrom, some for only the slightest reasons. I desire to review their work, so far as it treats of Marston, and to dispose of a large mass of conjecture which further investigation proves to be idle[1]. There remains, however, a certain number of facts, from which a fairly clear history of the whole matter can be drawn.

There are two considerations that narrow the personal importance of this stage-quarrel. First, its expression in the theatres depended very largely upon peculiar theatrical conditions; for a time these fostered quarrel-plays, but when the conditions changed, this kind of play was no longer possible.

Prof. Wallace has shown[2] that the Boys of Blackfriars were directly favoured and aided by Queen Elizabeth. "Their novel entertainments of music, singing, masque and drama under special favoring influences and select auditorial privileges, found that following that made them recognized as the foremost theatre in London. They became as a result the

[1] J. H. Penniman of the University of Pennsylvania wrote a monograph on the subject, 1887, which was followed two years later by a criticism in a larger monograph by R. A. Small. Fleay has contributed many random guesses. Lately Penniman has gone over the field again in his introduction to the *Belles Lettres* edition of Jonson's *Poetaster* and Dekker's *Satiromastix*. In addition, almost every writer on the Elizabethan drama has added a few conjectures or one or two facts.
[2] C. W. Wallace, *Children of the Chapel at Blackfriars*, 1908.

object of imitation and envy." He states furthermore that most Blackfriar plays imitated plays belonging to the other theatres. This quarrel of the companies was brought upon their stages; and it is to this rather than to the quarrel of the dramatists that Hamlet's words have reference: "There was for a while no money bid for argument unless the poet and the player went to cuffs in the question."[3] With the change of monarchs, special patronage to Blackfriars ceased, and consequently the reasons for public quarreling.

Secondly, critics have seen entirely too much personal satire in Elizabethan plays. This is particularly true in the case of Jonson. While he quarrelled often and bitterly, only one of his plays was directly inspired by a personal quarrel; and even in the *Poetaster* Jonson was almost more of a moralist than a controversalist. In several of Jonson's plays there are characters which represent Jonson himself, but even more definitely do they represent certain principles; and again and again his Brisks and Hedons represent a general type much more than they do any particular individual[4].

With these limitations in mind, we find nevertheless sure evidences of certain apparently bitter personal quarrels, which were fought out for the most part by proxy, and on the boards. Besides Jonson, Marston and Dekker, — Nash, Harvey, Monday, Lodge and others seem to have been participants; here only Marston's share will be considered.

Jonson twice refers to the beginning of his quarrel with Marston. In his conversations with Drummond, years later, Jonson is recorded to have said:

"He had many quarrels with Marston, beat him, and took his pistol from him, wrote his *Poetaster* on him; the beginning of them were that Marston represented him on the stage."[5]

[3] *Hamlet,* II ii, 340f. Dr. Wallace dates the passage late in 1601. See his *Children of the Chapel,* pp. 163f.

[4] Prof. Penniman has pointed out (Pref. to *Belles Lettres* Ed. of *Poet.* and *Satiro.*) that several of Jonson's sketches were drawn from *Wit's Misery* of Lodge; this is characteristic of his typical satiric method, borrowing from books rather than from life. For a discussion of the attributed attacks of Jonson on Daniel, see Baskerville, *English Elements in Jonson's Early Comedies,* p. 120.

[5] The concluding words of the sentence, "in his youth given to venery." probably are wrongly punctuated, and refer to what follows, not to Marston's quarrel. See Small for discussion.

21

In the *Apologetical Dialogue* appended to the *Poetaster*, Jonson wrote:

> "But sure I am, three years
> They did provoke me with their petulant styles
> On every stage; and I at last, unwilling
> But weary, I confess, of so much trouble,
> Thought I would try if shame could win upon em."

The *Dialogue* states it was "once spoken upon the stage," which must have been in 1601, when the *Poetaster* was produced. Thus the origin of the quarrel has been looked for in 1598. At that date none of Marston's work save his two volumes of satires had been published, consequently all early investigators sought to find in them an attack of Marston upon Jonson.

"Judicial Torquatus", with his "new-minted epithets, as reall, intrinsicate, Delphic," referred to in the Preface and Satire IX of the *Scourge of Villainy*, was first selected, by Gifford in 1816. This identification was taken for granted by Halliwell, Grosart, Bullen, Symonds and Penniman, until it was finally disproved by Small, who also showed that the licentious soldier Tubrio, the social aspirant Ruscus, and "Jack of Paris Garden" do not refer to Jonson[6]. There is no reference, then, to Jonson in Marston's formal satires; indeed, there is none to any dramatist or drama[7]. The failure to find the cause of the quarrel here, however, should only have been expected. In the first place, the satires were not produced on any stage. Furthermore, does Jonson's "three years" mean that the trouble started in 1598? The date of the *Poetaster* may be placed about June-July, 1601 — certainly the *Dialogue* was not written before that. Would not Jonson have counted 1601 as one

---

[6] H. C. Harte has shown that Torquatus in both passages means Gabriel Harvey (*N. & Q.* Ser. 9, vol. XI, pp. 201, 281, 343). Tubrio is in *S.* i and *S. V.* VII. He seems to have been identified with Jonson because both had 'rocky faces,' had been in the Low Countries, and were addicted to venery. But nowhere else is Jonson satirized at all in this fashion; Marston or Dekker never mention lust in his connection, but rail at him as a pedant. The connection with the parasite Ruscus (*S.* i.) is simply a conjecture of Grosart's, based on a similar device suggested in *Every Man Out*, I, i. Jack of Paris Garden was a well-known ape! (*S. V.* IX, 72.)

[7] Save for one reference to *Tamburlaine*.

of the three years? He obviously wished to appear to have been patient as long as possible. This would place the beginning of the quarrel in 1599, and in this year we find Marston producing one play, *Antonio and Mellida;* revising another, *Histriomastix;* and possibly collaborating in a third, *"Robert II, King of Scotte's Tragedy,"* now lost. It is in these plays, then, that I believe the seeds of the quarrel should be sought. Of these *Histriomastix* has been pointed out by Small.

HISTRIOMASTIX

This play contains the earliest dramatic work that can be assigned to Marston, and presents many points of doubt. We have but one edition, with a simple titlepage: HISTRIO-MASTIX. / Or, / THE PLAYER / whipt. / Printed for Th: Thorp. / 1610. Small, who has given it the most extensive treatment, calls it "a poor half-allegorical comedy." It begins as a tedious allegorical morality, with much undramatic philosophising. In the third act new elements of humour, satire and variety enter, obviously in Marston's style. Small's division of the play is for the most part correct; Marston contributed the part from III, iv to V, iii, and other scattered passages, altogether a little more than a quarter of the play[1]. The old *Histriomastix* has been dated by Small in the summer of 1596, on what seems to be sufficient evidence.

Concerning the authorship of the old *Histriomastix,* Simpson's[2] suggestion of Peele has been disproved by Small; who in turn suggests Chapman, because of certain similarities to his *Blind Beggar of Alexandria,* 1596, Chapman's first extant play. The *Blind Beggar* is the wildest extravaganza, in which one man plays three parts. It is improbable that an author's first two plays, produced in the same year, should be so utterly different as is the case here. None of the similarities noted by Small are distinctive, and there is no ring of Chapman's clearly marked style in the old *Histriomastix*[3].

[1] For more detailed division of authorship, see Appendix B.
[2] Simpson, *School of Shakespeare,* Vol. II, Introd. to *Histrio.*
[3] Small says the style of the two plays are similar: "monotonous, generally end-stopped lines, devoid of passion and spring" — which may be granted. That the general plan and subject-matter "are just what might be expected in an early dramatic effort of Chapman", is

Some resemblances to Dekker's *Old Fortunatus* exist[4], but the likenesses are less than the dissimilarities of tone, style and wording. It might be that Dekker had a hand with Marston in refurbishing the *Histriomastix*, and contributed a song, where there seems to be close similarity; but there is very little elsewhere.

Thomas Hariott, a philosopher and the most famous astronomer in England before Newton, was suggested to Simpson by the character of the academic philosopher Chrisoganus of the old play. Hariott, for long the protégé of Raleigh, was also the friend of Jonson and Chapman, and probably a member of the Mermaid club and Raleigh's free-thinking school, with Marlowe and Kyd[5]. The author may have had Hariott's character in mind when writing the play. We know of no purely literary production of Hariott himself.

Little is to be learnt of the author from his allusions to contemporary plays. Three passages in the older play have been paralleled in the works of Green, and one in those of Nash. There are references to *Tamburlaine, Gammer Gurton's Needle,* and apparently to *Midsummer Night's Dream*[6].

not substantiated by what we know of Chapman's work, which contains nothing else in this archaic form. Small admits the stanzaic structure form, marked by couplets or repeated lines, is not peculiar to Chapman; it would have been well known from passages in *Tamburlaine,* e. g. the "To entertain divine Zenocrate" passage. The parallels with the *Blind Beggar* have only a very general similarity. Chapman uses *hungerstarved,* but it was not uncommon in Elizabethan or later times (cf. *N. E. D.*)

[4] The blank verse refrain is found in *O. F.* several times (Shepherd's ed., 1873, pp. 84, 105-6, etc.) The closest resemblance is that of the harvesters' song at the end of Act I of *Histro.,* to two songs in *O. F.;* pp. 89, 173. Allegorical figures are used in much the same way, at times taking part in the action. There are a few verbal similarities.

But Dekker uses few Latin words or phrases, and always writes very clearly, while the old *Histrio,* is heavily Latinized, and often obscure in style.

[5] Boas, *Works of Kyd,* p. lxxi. *Life of Thomas Harriot,* by H. Stevens of Vermont. Privately printed, 1900.

[6] F. Hoppe, *Marston's Erstenwerke.* To *Midsummer Night's Dream,* cf. calling of the players' roll, I. ii, 130; players selecting their parts, near end of Act IV,; and V, v, 241. All that can be gathered from these references is that the author was somewhat conversant with current dramatic literature.

It is evident that the author must have been a scholar. The multiplicity of Latin words, names and quotations, and the dissertations of Chrisoganus on mathematics, astronomy and philosophy, indicate this more than sufficiently. I believe *Histriomastix* to have been a school play. It was obviously not a closet drama, but intended for acting. Being in part a satire on players, it would scarcely have been produced by an ordinary company. No children's companies were playing in 1596. The large number of songs[7] and of female parts[8] indicate that it was written for a boys' school rather than for a university.

The old *Histriamastix* was, in its general plan, a satire on the main classes of society; so the players do not refer to a particular company — the plan of the play requires a most general application. Chrisoganus, who is throughout held up as a model, and guide for society, may possibly have been drawn with Hariott in mind. It seems probable that Posthaste the hackwriter was meant as a type figure. If personal satire were intended, his original would be Anthony Monday. The original Posthaste is a former ballader (VI, v, 235) whom critics scorn for his extempore doggerel (II, v), and of whom a fellow-player says, "Is't not a pity this fellow's not employed in matters of state?" (II, 130). (Possibly some of this may have been inserted by Marston, to particularize Posthaste.) In general, then, the original play was a satire on society as a whole, written in something of the form of a morality, and not descending to personalities.

Marston's additions were probably made in 1599. They must have been acted in that year, because they are referred to in *Every Man Out*, acted about the turn of the years 1599-1600[9]. Small attempted to fix the date of *Histriomastix* in

[7] There are five songs and a morris in the remaining portion of the old play. (Small says six, but his list has three songs wrongly mentioned.) The portion replaced by Marston would have had several songs; he gives three and a masque: II, 247-55; 304-19; III, 78-9; VI, 288-95.

[8] In the first act eight female and five male figures are all on the stage at once, something impossible for an ordinary company. Marston's additional ending, written for a children's company, employed a considerably greater number of female characters simultaneously.

[9] Cf. infra, p. 31, n. 1.

25

August, 1599, because of the line, "The Spaniards are coming," but this line cannot be restricted to any month or year; it could never have been meaningless during the latter part of Elizabeth's reign. However, Jonson would not have selected an old play to satirize. Furthermore, the number of songs and female parts indicate a children's company, and this would probably have been the Children of Paul's, who presented all of Marston's other plays written before 1603; if so, the earliest date possible is 1599[10].

When Marston's personal satire in the play is examined, it is found to be individualized only in the characters of Chrisoganus and Posthaste. Marston quite alters the character of Chrisoganus. He early introduces into the midst of older material (II, 63-7) a passage which shows the academical philosopher and eminently harmless stoic in a new light:

> "How, you translating scholar. you can make
> A stabbing satire or an epigram,
> And think you carry just Rhamnusia's whip,
> To lash the patient; go, get you clothes,
> Our free-born blood such apprehension loathes."

The main part of Marston's additions to the play begins with another treatment of the new Chrisoganus (III, 180). He demands of the players the large sum of ten pounds for writing a play for them, and when refused flies into an unphilosophical rage. The old play never presents Chrisoganus as a dramatist.

The other appearances of Marston's Chrisoganus only enlarge on this same character of pedantic satirist. In IV, ii he bursts into curses of "this idiot world that comforts all

[10] The first mention of Paul's Children is in Marston's *Jack Drum*, which they produced in 1600, (V, 102-4) :

> "I saw the children of Paul's last night . . .
> The apes in time. will do it handsomely."

A little later they are said to have played, previously, "Musty fopperies of antiquity," which sounds much like *Histrio*. I see no reason why their revival should not have dated from the previous year, 1599. It is of course possible, though not very probable considering all his other early plays, that Marston should have revised *Histrio*. for the Children of the Chapel, which Wallace believes began their revival with Johnson's *Case Is Altered*, Sept.-Oct., 1597; (*Children of the Chapel*, p. 58.)

saving industrious art"; in V, iii (103) he tries to act as peacemaker to the quarrelsome nobles, and receives for his reward, "Peace, prating scholar!... A pox upon this linguist, take him hence."

Thus Marston found a stoic, scientific, not very individualized philosopher, the personification of Wisdom crying out in the streets, and no man regarding. In Marston's hands, this calm servant of the Muses becomes a railing satirist, rating his own plays very highly while abusing those of others.

There seem to have been three sources for this character. One is the older Chrisoganus, whom Marston has carried over especially in his academic traits. So in IV, ii, he bewails the decay of learning,

> "whilst pale Artizans
> Pine in the shades of gloomy Academes,
> Faint in pursuit of virtue, and quite tired
> For want of liberal food for liberal art,
> Give up the goal to sluggish ignorance!"

Oftener he is a representative of Marston instead of the unknown scholarly dramatist. So in V, iii:

> "Now is the time wherein . . .
> Pity and Piety are both exiles,
> Religion buried with our fathers' bones,
> In the cold earth, and nothing but her face
> Left to adorn these gross and impious times . . .
> Justice hath whips to scourge impiety."

This is quite in the frame of mind of Marston's satires, — how evil are these times!

Finally, Chrisoganus possesses a few traits that seem to have more special contemporary reference. He is called "translating scholar"; "you can make a stabbing satire or an epigram"; you think yourself to be Nemesis herself; "go, get you clothes." Meanwhile he demands "ten pound a play"; he calls his own poetry "rich invention", "sweet smooth lines held precious"; he constantly despises "this common beast the multitude." Here it seems that Marston had Ben Jonson in mind. The most frequent charges against Jonson were that he was arrogant, full of self-conceit, had poor clothes, satirized society, was exactly a "translating scholar". He himself says of Horace-Jonson in the *Poetaster*, that he is accused of "his self-love, his arrogancy and his impudence in commending his own things and his translating."[12] The only other person who has been suggested for the model is Marston himself[13]; we have seen that part of the portrait seemed to express his feelings, but he was no translator, nor poor, nor, so far as we know, did he write arrogantly, but rather with perhaps too much outward humility[14].

If it be Jonson at whom the character of Chrisoganus was aimed — and it seems almost certain — in what spirit was it written? On the whole, evidently in one of praise. He may be called the hero of the play, the only high-souled character shown. The play, as the title indicates, was directed chiefly against the adult players, and especially Monday, whom Jonson was also satirizing in *The Case is Altered* and *Every Man In;* so far Marston would be acting as an ally.

But Chrisoganus is shown to be exactly what Jonson is; he is attacked as well as praised; and we know from the *Poetaster* and elsewhere that Jonson did not view himself in a well-balanced way, but was almost absurdly arrogant. Marston took the old unreal morality figure, and turned it into a satirist and dramatist, with sharp temper and great arrogance. He shows how Pride attacked the characters of the play, including Chrisoganus: puffed up with a sense of his own worth Chrisoganus demands an extraordinary price for a play, and falls into a rage when he fails to succeed. Quite aside from general satire, it seems very probable that we have

[12] Chrisoganus, when under the influence of Envy, talks just as Macilente does in *Every Man Out* — an example of the close connection in tone between Jonson and Marston. Baskerville (pp. 298-9) has collected a considerable number of parallels between *Histrio.* and the *Poetaster,* showing the probability of some conscious or unconscious connection.

Penniman suggests (Introd. *Poetaster*, p. xlvii) that Marston is putting into Chrisoganus' mouth, the charges Jonson had made against Monday (Antonio Balladino), in *The Case is Altered.*

[13] Simpson (*School of Shakespeare*, II, Introd. to *Histrio.*) was the first critic to give this play any special attention. He believed that Chrisoganus was meant to represent Marston himself, but with Jonson as an ideal, and hence borrowing many Jonsonian traits. But C. is not altogether an ideal character.

[14] Save here and there in the satires, where his role demanded imperiousness.

here a mischievous caricaturing of some special incident in Jonson's career as a playwright[15]. Marston would be quite capable of showing both sides of Jonson; apparently praising him, by showing him as a learned and good man, and at the same time exposing his failings. Jonson would need no more incitement to quarrel; he had not altered his characteristics when, a score of years later, Drummond wrote of him (Jan., 1616):

"He is a great lover and praiser of himself — thinketh nothing well but that either he himself or some of his friends or countrymen hath said or done — jealous of every word and action of those about him; he is passionately kind and angry — interpreteth best sayings and deeds often to the worst."

I believe that this rather ambiguous characterization was the starting-point of the whole stage-quarrel. Marston very probably did not expect such a result. Judging from their reconciliations and from the tone of passages which Marston seems to have inspired in *Satiromastix*[16], Marston had a sincere liking for the "passionately kind and angry" Jonson. But when Marston's satiric, saturnine, observing disposition coupled with his genuine ability as a writer met Jonson's suspicious temper and arrogance, conflict was inevitable. It is interesting to imagine the circumstances of the scene when burly Ben "beat him, took his pistol from him", with Jonson's English sturdiness contrasted to Marston's Italian strain.

Marston's Posthaste has been thought by some to be intended for Shakespeare[17]. Their case rests on a line in the burlesque interlude of Troilus and Cressida (II, 273):

"That when he *shakes* his furious *Speare,*"

where we have a conjunction of the name of Shakespeare and that of one of his plays. However, the facts show it to be a coincidence. It takes bold guesswork to place any of

[15] Baskerville (p. 302f.) suggests Jonson's disgrace in connection with his trouble over the *Isle of Dogs*. That he was 'provoked for three years on every stage' may indicate lampooning arising from this. Histriomastix might present a burlesque of this quarrel between Jonson and the players. Jonson, ashamed of the *Isle of Dogs*, might well resent such a half-favorable reference to it. Crispinus in *Poet.* is made the poet for players, like Chrisoganus in this play.

[16] Cf. infra, p. 73f.

[17] Simpson, *School of Shakespeare;* H. Wood, *Am. J. Phil.* XVI, 3.

the Shakespearean work on *Troilus and Cressida* before 1599. The resemblance of the interlude is anything but close to the passage in *Troilus and Cressida* (V, ii) with which it is usually compared. What was parodied was probably a *Troilus and Cressida* now lost, on which Dekker and Chettle were engaged by Henslowe in April-May, 1599. Numerous examples of the coincidence of *shake* and *spear* in literature have been collected by Small and Hoppe, none of which can possibly refer to Shakespeare.

It is much more probable that Posthaste was intended for Monday. In the older part of the play we have seen that the characteristics of the two were not unlike. Marston adds much that is particular; what we know of Monday so closely corresponds that the personal satire seems established[18].

Marston did not alter the older writer's conception of the players[19]. The old author did not think much of the dramatic profession, and let it be seen; Marston was writing for a children's company, and so was at liberty to berate the common players.

It is probable that "Mr. Maxton, the new poet" of Henslowe's diary was Marston; it is quite possible, as Small surmises, that the unnamed play for which he was paid was *Robert II, King of Scotte's Tragedy*. If so, we find Marston collaborating with Jonson and two others in September, 1599 — in itself not at all unlikely[20].

Both parts of *Antonio and Mellida* we know to have been on the stage in 1599[21], but there was no further satire on any dramatist in these plays as first acted[22]. Indeed, Marston copied some of the humours Jonson had made popular in his first Humour play.

[18] For parallels, see Small, *Stage Quarrel*, p. 173 f.

[19] The only instance of much individuality is in the players' song preceding the Troilus interlude, with its mention of the three and four companies. Too much stress should not be put upon the words of an obscure song.

[20] About the same time Dekker and Jonson were collaborating on the *Page of Plymouth*.

[21] Wallace cannot be far wrong when he dates *A. and M.* in the first half of 1599, and *A's. R.* in November.

[22] Cf. infra, Appendix D.

Jonson's retort to what he rightly or wrongly considered
the insult of the Chrisoganus, was in this his next play, which
was produced about the end of the century[1]. Two characters
in the play have commonly been spoken of as intended to
represent Marston — Carlo Buffone and Clove. I believe
neither identification is correct. That of Carlo Buffone is still
in dispute[2], and there are difficulties in any identification of
the character with a single person. The most prominent
characteristic of Carlo is that he is "a public, scurrilous and
profane jester;" "no honorable or reverend person whatsoever can come within reach of his eye, but is turned into all
manner of variety, by his adulterate similes."

> "O, 'tis an open-throated, black-mouthed cur,
> That bites at all, but eats on those that feed him."[3]

His second most important characteristic is that he is a
great glutton and wine-bibber, and plays the toady to be
invited to supper. Everyone fears him for his wit, and
despises him for his lack of heart. Carlo fears the quick
saturnine spirit of Macilente, who in turn "hates him as he
hates the devil".

The principal reason for the identification of Carlo with
Marston is a line in II, i, where Puntarvolo addresses him,
"Thou grand Scourge, or Second Untruss of the Time."
It will be remembered that Hall's *Virgidemiarum*, or

---

[1] The play speaks of being acted in the spring, and of "this year
of jubilee coming on". J., after his slow habit, "scarce a play a year,"
had presumably been working on this play ever since he had finished
Every Man In, in the autumn of 1598. Cf. Baskerville, p. 144, n. 2:
"E. M. O. was doubtless finished toward the end of 1599, N. S."
Wallace, *Child. of Chapel,* dates it "ca. Aug. '99."

[2] Fleay has identified Carlo as both Marston (*Chr.* I, 97) and Dekker (I, 360). Marston has been named by Herford in *D. N. B.*, Symonds, Penniman and Schelling (*Eliz. Dra.* I, 481; 1907.) Small
(*Stage Quarrel*) after Gifford suggested Charles Chester as the
original, and has convinced Thorndike (*Camb. Hist. Eng. Lit.*, VI,
Ch. ii) and partially Schelling (*Everyman ed.* of Jonson, I, p. xiv,
1910.) Bullen named Dekker (*D. N. B.*)

[3] *In Every Man Out,* Carlo is described in the Character of Persons prefixed to the play; toward the end of the Prologue; the play
passim, especially I, i; IV, iv; V. iv, where his lips are sealed with
wax.

'harvest of rods', was followed by the *Scourge of Villainy* by Marston, who thus became in a sense the second English satirist, scourge, or 'untruss' of the time[4]. But this is almost the only likeness between Carlo and Marston, while there are many differences; Carlo, for instance, was not in any way connected with the stage or literature, and in no way resembles Jonson's later avowed portrait of Marston in Crispinus. Does not the line in question mean simply that, as Marston had been widely known for his *Scourge of Villainy*, so Carlo was a second such figure, in that he railed at everyone? At any rate, the differences in the characters are so great that if there be any identity, which I doubt, it must be only a momentary one. I believe that Carlo partly is drawn from the figure of Charles Chester, and partly is simply a type, one of Jonson's Humour-characters[5].

[4] Marston does not use the word untruss or untrusser, but at the end of S. V. IX he wrote:
"I'll strip you nak't, and whip you with my rhymes,
Causing your shame to live to after-times."

[5] The arguments against Chester are not so strong as those for him. Aubrey, sometimes over-credulous, in his *Life of Raleigh* (II, 184) said:
"From Dr. Pell: In his youthful time, was one Charles Chester, that often kept company with his acquaintance; he was a bold impertinent fellow, and they could never be quiet for him; a perpetual talker, and made a noise like a drum in a room. So one time in a tavern Sir W. R. beats him and seals up his mouth [i. e. his upper and nether beard] with hard wax. From him Ben Jonson takes his Carlo Buffone in *Every Man Out of His Humour.*"

The objections of Gifford can be answered. In Raleigh's youth Jonson was very young; but "In his youthful time" may refer not to Raleigh, but to Pell. Even though the incident had occurred a score of years before *E. M. O.* it would not be unlike Jonson to adopt it. Chester was well known at the end of the century — he is mentioned twice in Harrington's *Metamorphosis of Ajax*. Gifford could see no likeness between Chester and Carlo; to me they seem remarkably alike.

If Carlo be drawn from Chester, at least in part, it does not necessarily follow that Puntarvolo, who seals Carlo's mouth, is taken from Raleigh. On this matter cf. Hart's ed. of *Jonson*, I, xxxviif.; II, ixf. Penniman, ed. of *Poetaster*, p. lv. Small, *Stage Quarrel*, pp. 36, 47. Baskerville, p. 174-5, 197n.

In the Dedication to *Volpone* Jonson seems to admit doing something similar to using Chester: "Where have I been particular? where personal? except to a mimic, cheater, bawd or *buffon?*"

Is it not possible that Johnson was intending a pun: Carlo Buffone, Charles Jester, (Chester)?

It frequently has been declared that Clove and Orange represent Marston and Dekker, whereas in reality they are only type figures. They are best described by Cordatus in the only scene in which they appear, III, ii:

"A couple, sir, that are mere strangers to the whole scope of our play . . . . 'Tis as dry an Orange as ever grew: nothing but salutation, and O Lord, sir, and, It pleases you to say so, sir! one that can laugh at a jest for company with a most plausible and extemporal grace; and some hour after in private ask you what it was. The other monsieur, Clove, is a more spiced youth; he will sit you a whole afternoon sometimes, in a bookseller's shop, reading the Greek, Italian, and Spanish, when he understands not a word of either."

Clove exemplifies this, by talking three nonsense sentences filled with big words, when he is in the hearing of some auditors. Two of the sentences use no especially Marstonian words; but the second of the three runs as follows (words especially used by Marston italicised):

CLOVE. Now, sir, whereas the ingenuity of the time and the soul's *synderisis* are but embrions in nature, added to the *paunch of Esquiline*, and the intervallum of the *Zodiac*, besides the *ecliptic* line being optic, and not mental, but by the *contemplative* and theoric part thereof, doth *demonstrate* to us the vegetable *circumferance*, and the ventuosity of the *tropics*, and whereas our *intellectual*, or *mincing capreal* (according to the metaphysics) as you may read in Plato's *Histriomastix* — You conceive me, sir?
ORANGE. O lord, sir!"

It is easy to perceive how Clove represents pretentious ignorance, and Orange the absence of any thought at all. It is these general types that Jonson is presenting. They are given no personal characteristics save the one trait Jonson wished to satirize. Even the language Clove uses was not meant primarily to satirize Marston, for his first and last paragraphs contain only three long words found in Marston, and those not uncommon ones[6]. Indeed, when the words distinctively Marstonian, and so likely to be used in ridiculing him, are sought, they are reduced to two phases, *paunch of*

[6] *Meteors, mathematical* and *Pythagorical* (only *Pythagoras* is found in Marston). In the third paragraph, in which these occur, is to be found also a reference to Shakespeare's *Julius Caesar*, III, ii; "Oh, judgment! thou art fled to brutish beasts."

Esquiline and *mincing capreal,* and two words, *synderisis,* and *intellectual* used as a noun. None of the words in this passage did Jonson in the *Poetaster* cause Crispinus-Marston to disgorge save *ventuosity* — and that has not been discovered in Marston's works.

Jonson, looking about for long words to fill up the pretentious patter-speech of Clove, evidently thought of Marston's recent play *Histriomastix,* which, like all of Marston's work, had a peculiar vocabulary, — even the title was a word such as Jonson was seeking. Besides, there was a chance of paying back for Chrisoganus, whom Marston had made somewhat like Jonson, and then called "Prating scholar", and told "Go, get you clothes!" So it would be natural for Jonson to use from *Histriomastix* such unusual words as he might remember, and even go to the *Scourge of Villainy* and pick out a few strange words[7]. To make the reference certain, and because the word fitted his purpose, he even used the title, *Histriomastix.*

Thus he struck a blow at Marston in passing, but this was not the reason for his creation of Clove and Orange, nor was what little character they have, derived from Marston or Dekker[8].

JACK DRUM'S ENTERTAINMENT

The next phase of the quarrel is to be found in *Jack Drum's Entertainment*[1], which was produced in 1600, the year after

[7] Especially from *Satires* VIII-X. There are eight words from *Histriomastix* (mostly from the non-Marstonian astronomy of the first act) and eight from the *Scourge of Villainy;* though the three in the last paragraph may not be from Marston at all.

Small argues that Jonson was not aiming at Marston since words from the old *Histrio.* are used. But Jonson would not pick and choose between different parts of the play; indeed he probably was ignorant of the older school-play.

[8] There is no reason to believe Jonson and Dekker were at odds as early as this; had they been, the only reason for believing that Orange represented Dekker is that he is the companion of Clove-Marston. We do not know of Marston's and Dekker's relations at this time.

[1] Bullen excludes *J. D.* and *Histrio* from his edition of Marston only because 'they are of little value and easily accessible' (I, p. lii, n.), scarcely sufficient reasons. The text used for these two plays is that of Simpson's *School of Shakespeare,* compared with *facsimile* reprints.

Histriomastix and *Every Man Out*[2]. It was published anonymously, but there can be no doubt of Marston's authorship, so plain is his marked style and vocabulary[3]. Critics have made numerous guesses at the originals of some of the characters, for the most part without any basis of fact.

Some of the characteristics of Brabant Senior were intended as a hit at Jonson. Brabant was a rather foolish, well-to-do man, whose chief delight was in gathering about him those at whom he could laugh. He is the practical joker who shows off the weak sides of his companions. Near the end of the first act he says:

"Why, this is sport imperial, by my gentry! I would spend forty crowns, for such another feast of fools . . . Why, 'tis the recreation of my intellect . . . . These are my zanies; I fill their paunches, they feel my pleasures; I use them as my fools, faith, ha, ha!"

He is conceited, and dislikes all "our modern wits"; thus he detracts, when the company are praising the Children of Pauls:

"Aye, and if they had good plays. But they produce
Such musty fopperies of antiquity,
And do not suit the humorous age's backs
With clothes of fashion.
PLANET. Well, Brabant, well, you will be censuring still.
There lies a jest in steep, will whip you for't."[4]

This jest comes at the end of the play. Brabant becomes a self-made cuckold, after setting John fo de King to attempt Brabant's wife, in whose chastity he mistakenly trusts. Planet forces a horned hat upon Brabant, saying:

[2] It is dated from references to the Irish rebellion and especially to leapyear ("What! 'tis woman's year!" — I, 66).

[3] Simpson, and Small (*Stage Quarrel*, pp. 94-5) have given sufficient evidence of Marston's authorship. Many of the words Jonson ridicules in the *Poet.* are found only in *J. D. E.* among Marston's works. A few parallels to Marston not before given are: Introd., 25-6: *W. Y. W.*, II, i, 51. I, 162: *S. V.* III, 25. I, 222; *S. V.* IX, 56, *A. & M.* II, i, 151. I, 346; *Sat.* iii, 81.; |I, 123: *A. & M.* III, ii, 188. I, 427: *W. Y. W.* II, i, 72-3, III, 64f: cf. Laverdure in *W. Y. W.* II, i, esp. 1. 157. IV, 124: *A. R.* II, ii, 219.

[4] V, 102. In Brabant's words Marston seems to be alluding to some criticism of Jonson upon *Histriomastix*.

"Why dost thou not well deserve to be thus used?
Why should'st thou take felicity to gull
Good honest souls, and in thy arrogance
And glorious ostentation of thy wit,
Think God infused all perfection
Into thy soul alone, and made the rest
For thee to laugh at? Now, you Censurer,
Be the ridiculous subject of our mirth.
Why, fool, the power of Creation
Is still omnipotent, and there's no man that breathes
So valiant, learned, witty, or so wise,
But it can equal him out of the same mould
Wherein the first was formed. Then leave proud scorn,
And, honest self-made cuckold, wear the horn."

One of Jonson's prominent characteristics in his humour comedies is his lack of sympathy with almost all of those he portrays. The only ones whom he depicts favorably are those who draw out fools or persons with humours, and make them appear ridiculous. It is natural for a dramatist to ally himself with knowledge and wit against folly; but Jonson does this in a particularly heartless way, coldly and in what would be an almost inhuman manner if his gulls were felt to be alive, instead of being, for the most part, only careful mechanical constructions of the dramatist's able brain. The character of Brabant Senior in *Jack Drum's Entertainment* is aimed against this aspect of Jonson's plays. Brabant is made as foolish as his dupes, and Marston takes their side against him, making him fall into the pit that he digged for others. I do not believe that the figure of Brabant Senior on the stage was intended to bring the figure of Jonson before the eyes of the audience; but Marston was combating a literary device of Johnson's, and more than that, a real and fundamental failing — lack of human sympathy. The play was not intended to imply that Ben Jonson went about London with a train of simpletons, in order to amuse himself; but it attacked Jonson because he apparently sympathised with those of his characters who on the stage did just that[5]. A part of the last speech quoted:

[5] Marston was taking the same stand as Sidney: "and the great fault, even in that point of laughter, and forbidden plainly by Aristotle, is that they stir laughter in sinful things, which are rather execrable than ridiculous; or in miserable, which are rather to be pitied than scorned." (*Defense of Poesie*, Cook, p. 51).

36

> "Why should'st thou . . .
> in thy arrogance
> And glorious ostentation of thy wit,
> Think God infused all perfection
> Into thy soul alone, and made the rest
> For thee to laugh at?",

might have been intended to apply directly to Jonson *in propria persona*, in reference to the magniloquent introduction to the *Every Man out of his Humour*.

In brief, Marston did not put Jonson himself on the stage, or satirize him personally, in the person of Brabant Senior. What he did was to rebuke Jonson for a characteristic of his dramas, and incidentally satirize his arrogance, and his disdain for contemporary literature[6].

Many guesses have been made as to the meaning of the minor characters. Planet seems to represent the author. He is a representative of the Malcontent type, discontented with life in general, and delighted in exposing its pettiness. He is not intended, of course, to be Marston, but simply to express his views of life. In general, he represents the norm of reason, from which the other characters more or less widely depart. It is evident he is largely modeled on Jonson's Macilente.

Several critics have asserted that Marston is portraying himself in Young Brabant[7]. The only grounds for this belief are in a single passage (I, 227-32):

> "Indeed young Brabant is a proper man;
> And yet his legs are somewhat of the least;
> And, faith, a chitty, well-complexioned face;
> And yet it wants a beard; a good sweet youth . . ."

Crispinus-Marston also has little legs; but he has a red beard. Besides, Young Brabant is a jilted and rather foolish lover, of the type Marston so often satirized.

There is a passage in the fourth act (II, 37f.) where Brabant Senior depreciates the poets of the day[8]. He heads

---

[6] Cf. *infra*.

Fleay and Simpson believe that Brabant Senior was meant for Hall. But it was not that kind of scourging satire that Marston was attacking in this play, but rather that which displayed the foolish without sympathy.

[2] Simpson, *School of Shakespeare*, II, 129; Fleay, *Chr.* II, 74; Penniman, *War*, 72.

[8] Cf. the idea of the opening of the *II Return from Parnassus; infra*, p. 79.

the list with "the new poet Mellidus", where he is probably referring to Marston himself, as author of *Antonio and Mellida*. In what is perhaps an adaptation of some criticism of Jonson, he calls him "a slight bubbling spirit, a cork, a husk."

Musus in this passage has been called either Chapman, who finished Marlowe's *Hero and Leander,* taken from Museaus; or Daniel, whom Drayton[9] called "the sweet Museaus of these times." These are simply guesses, as is the one which links the Decius of the passage with Drayton, simply because he is so denominated in an epigram (not entered till 1610) of John Davies. Not enough is said about any of these poets, save perhaps Mellidus, to identify them with any contemporary, if indeed Marston had particular men in mind.

Fleay has a mass of conjectures regarding this play, for few of which he has anything like proof. He supposes Jonson to be indicated in the character of John fo de King, partly I suppose because of the similarity of names; and partly because Jonson told Drummond "that a man made his own wife to court him [i. e., Jonson], whom he enjoyed two years ere he knew of it, and one day finding them by chance, was passingly delighted with it", while John fo de King was invited by Brabant Senior to court Brabant's wife, in jest, but the courting proved too successful. John was a Frenchman whose whole aim in life was lust. Penniman, who argues in favor of the identification, admits too much when he says:

"Although to us the character of Monsieur John fo de King does not seem to resemble Jonson, yet stage 'business' and mimicry were possibly introduced in presenting these plays, so that to the audience it was perfectly clear who was represented."

No 'business' or mimicry could have made John, with his accent, his constant offers to 'teach French' and his burning lust, into the scholar and poet Jonson[10].

[9] In *Endimion and Phoebe,* 1594.

[10] Penniman further says (p. 71): "Marston probably refers to the attack made on him in the 'fustian' conversation between Clove and Orange, when he makes Planet say: 'By the Lord, fustian, now I understand it: compliment is as much as fustian.'" (III, 87.) There is absolutely no allusion to *Every Man Out* in this chance use of the word fustian, which is clearly prepared for and called out by the context. It is such dragging in of far-fetched allusions which do not allude to anything, that makes some criticism on the stage-quarrel so ridiculous.

Fleay identifies Sir Edward Fortune, the care-free revelling father, with Edward Alleyn, who was that year building the Fortune theatre. But the name Fortune seems to be significant only of the knight's wealth and disposition[11]. Mammon he connects with Henslowe, because Mammon is a usurer who is hated by the people. But Mammon is a Jew; the original list of characters includes "7. Mammon the usurer, with a great nose."[12]

Such a nest of conjecture as the following can only proceed from a wrong conception of the part played by personal satire in Elizabethan drama: "Timothy Tweedle seems very like Anthony Monday, and Christopher Flawn I take to be Christopher Beeston. John Ellis, with his similies, is a gross caricature of John Lily . . . Pasquil is perhaps Nicholas Breton" or Nashe[13]. Few if any plays were cryptogramic mosaics such as this would indicate. It was only the exceptional Elizabethan play which contained any personal satire, and such satire was almost always limited to a few characters. Audiences could not have been expected to recognize the foibles, more or less disguised, of a dozen authors.

[11] Cf., in other plays of Marston, the names of Feliche, Bilioso, Malheureaux, and many of the characters in the *Fawn*. Fortune was an elderly father; Alleyn at the time was only thirty-four, and childless. The passage given to Fortune, disdaining to "lean upon the vulgar's rotten love," could not have referred to a popular actor.

[12] Fleay believes Sordido in *Every Man Out* to be Henslowe. This Small disproves. For Mammon's nose, cf. II, 328f.

[13] Fleay. No disproof is needed, because no proof can be given, of these identifications of Tweedle and Flawn. The name John Ellis is somewhat like John Lily, but Ellis' foolish similes are not built after the pattern of the similes of *Euphues*.

The word Pasquil is equivalent to Pasquin, meaning lampooner or satirist, which is not at all the character of Pasquil in the play; he is simply the ardent, at times frantic lover of Katherine. Nash sometimes wrote under the name of Pasquil, and may have died in this year, 1600. But the fact that Pasquil in the play is supposed to be dead, and that Katharine talks of his ghost, (II, 233) does not necessarily imply that Nash is referred to, as Small would have it, (p. 100).

If a personal reference is needed at all, Pasquil would seem rather to refer to Nicholas Breton, who in this same year published four books whose titles all contained the word *"Pasquil's"*. But Pasquil in the play is not much individualized; I think his name was merely the adoption of a popular phrase, as was *Jack Drum's Entertainment*.

Jack Drum's Entertainment, then, represents a distinct attack upon a dramatic practice of Jonson's, with incidental references to certain of his personal characteristics. But no one, I believe, was really brought upon the stage in recognizable likeness to Jonson.

CYNTHIA'S REVELS

The next play to be considered for its bearing on the course of the stage-quarrel is the *Cynthia's Revels* of Jonson, which was acted probably a little later than *Jack Drum's Entertainment*. Neither play refers to the other, and they were probably composed at about the same time.[1] *Cynthia's Revels* is a satire on court manners. Two characters only engage our attention: Anaides and Hedon; each of these has been said by various critics to represent either Marston or Dekker. Both Anaides and Hedon, however, I consider to have represented for the most part types, without personal satire.

The more commonly accepted interpretation is that Marston is brought on the stage in the character of Hedon, and Dekker in that of Anaides. The main proof advanced is a quotation of the *Cynthia's Revels* in *Satiromastix*. Johnson had written (*C. R.* III, ii):

> "But when I remember
> 'Tis Hedon and Anaides, alas, then
> I think but what they are, and am not stirred.
> The one a light voluptuous reveler,
> The other, a strange arrogating puff,
> Both impudent and arrogant enough."

Dekker wrote in *Satiromastix* (I, ii, 183):

> "HORACE. That same Crispinus [i. e., Marston] is the silliest dor, and Fannius [i. e., Dekker] the slightest cobweb-lawn piece of a poet, oh God!

[1] Wallace dates it April-May, 1600 (*Children of Chapel*); Baskerville (p. 214n), the winter of 1600-1; Small (p. 24), Feb.-Mar. 1601, N. S. Nearly a thousand additional lines appeared in the folio of 1616, that had not been in the quarto of 1601. Baskerville (p. 227) believes these lines to have been in the original acting version, but this view is successfully opposed by Judson in his edition of *Cynthia's Revels* in the *Yale Studies* (p. x). The lines in question will not be taken up here. The references are to Judson's edition.

Why should I care what every dor doth buzz
In credulous ears; it is a crown to me,
That the best judgments can report me wronged.
ASINIUS. I am one of them that can report it.
HOR. 'I think but what they are, and am not moved,
    The one a light voluptuous reveler,
    The other a strange arrogating puff,
    Both impudent and arrogant enough.'
ASI. S'lid, do not Criticus revel in these lines, ha, ningle, ha?
HOR. Yes, they're my own."

Jonson's lines clearly make Hedon the 'reveler' and Anaides the 'puff'. Most critics have likewise taken for granted that Dekker's lines make Crispinus (Marston) the 'reveler' and Fannius (Dekker) the 'puff'. But this is by no means certain. Six lines intervene between the mention of the names, and that of their attributes; the original speaker has been interrupted by another. The quotation from *Cynthia's Revels* seems to be in a rather different train of thought and not connected closely with the mention of Crispinus and Fannius. Even if some reference does exist, in such a hastily written play the order of names, 'Crispinus and Fannius', may well have been inverted in the quotation of 'reveler and puff'. At the best, these passages cannot bear the entire weight of the identification, as Small, for example, in his elaborate treatment of the point, assumes.[2]

It may be taken for granted that Jonson meant Crites, the speaker of the lines in *Cynthia's Revels,* to represent, not exactly Jonson himself, but the ideal critic, imbued with Jonson's ideals, and acting as Jonson would have desired to act. Attacks on him would be understood to be attacks on Jonson.

Hedon is twice described in the play at some length—in the Induction, and near the beginning of Act II. He is a courtier *par excellence,* 'a gallant wholly consecrated to his pleasures.' He has little money, but makes a great show, with fine clothes and 'a fencer, a pedant and a musician seen in his lodgings a-mornings'. He courts ladies with telling of his exploits in the mock tournaments; he is always over-

---

[2] Judson (*Cyn. Rev.* p. 71) think that Dekker did not intend any identification when introducing the passage, but was merely ridiculing "the pompous egoism of Crites-Horace-Jonson". This is quite probable.

41

perfumed.   Naturally he is opposed to the sham-hating Crites, of whom he says (IV, v, 50) :

"I wonder the fellow does not hang himself, being thus scorn'd and contemned of us that are held the most accomplished society of gallants . . . I protest, if I had no music in me, no courtship, that I were not a reveler and could dance, or had not those excellent qualities that give a man life and perfection, but a mere poor scholar as he is, I think I should make some desperate way with myself; whereas now — would I might never breathe more, if I do know that creature in this kingdom with whom I would change."

We have one picture which Jonson drew avowedly of Marston—Crispinus in the Poetaster.   The best test of whether Hedon be intended to satirize Marston is to compare Hedon and Crispinus; and we shall find the likeness small. Hedon is an assured courtier, and apparently little else; Crispinus is "a gentleman born", to be sure, but he is a newcomer to court, who is able to say nothing save to commend others' jests.   Hedon does not seem to be worried about money, has a retinue and fine clothes; Crispinus is poor, pursued by bailiffs, and threadbare.   They are both rhymers rather than poets; but Crispinus intends to be a poet, while Hedon disdains the name as unbecoming to a courtier.   Nowhere in the play does Hedon use any suggestion of Crispinus' style.   Jonson had already noted the oddity of Marston's vocabulary (in *Every Man Out*) : had he intended a portrayal of Marston, would he not at least once have used a Marstonian expression, or at any rate some of his model's harshness of manner?   Hedon, with his "By the tip of your ear, sweet lady" — "By the white valley that lies between the alpine hills of your bosom, I protest—", is the exact opposite.   Both Hedon and Crispinus sing; but in a play written for presentation by a Childrens' Company, very little can be inferred from that.   Both Hedon and Crispinus are contemptuous of the character standing for Jonson; but they take quite a different attitude toward him: Hedon scorns and contemns him, while Crispinus desires to be friendly with him, and only when he is repulsed becomes his enemy.   Hedon and Anaides, though unlike, are social equals, and friendly; Crispinus is familiar with Demetrius, but superior to him.

Thus the only important likeness is that both Hedon and Crispinus belong to pairs of characters who are enemies of

Jonson (in so far as he puts himself into his plays). This does not of course aid in distinguishing Hedon from Anaides. A fairly good case has been made out for the identification of Hedon with Daniel[3]; at any rate he is much more probably Daniel than Marston. Had it not been for the *Satiromastix* lines, no one would have picked out Hedon as representing Marston. The truth of the matter seems to be that Hedon was primarily intended as a satire on a type of courtier, closely corresponding to Fastidious Brisk and Marston's Castilio— the elegant, dapper courtier who is somewhat effeminate. Some traits of Daniel may have been in Jonson's mind; but there was no reference to Marston, or to Dekker.

There is somewhat more doubt concerning the significance of Anaides, because he is not such an utter opposite to Marston as was Hedon. He is fully described in the Induction and II, i. He is more of the ordinary gallant than the courtier, though "he has two essential parts of the courtier, pride and ignorance . . . 'Tis Impudence itself, Anaides." He jests brazenly, and is extremely blasphemous. He has had land come to him by chance; he will give no money to a friend in need, but "Marry, to his cockatrice or punquetto, half a dozen taffeta gowns or satin kirtles in a pair or two of months, why, they are nothing." He is said by other courtiers (IV, i 33f.) to have 'a small voice, a very imperfect face, hands too great, by at least a straw's breadth, and they say he puts off the calves of his legs, with his stockings, every night'. He hates Crites, despises him because he is a scholar, and fears him on account of his satire.

What resemblances can be found in Anaides to Crispinus or to what is otherwise known of Marston? His name, Impudence, reminds one of Crispinus thrusting himself upon Horace; but that incident was only adapted from Horace, and the types of impudence are different — one overbearing, the other servile. Anaides is not the absolute courtier, as was Hedon, but an arrogant and ignorant gallant; in this he is somewhat nearer Crispinus. He 'speaks all that comes in his cheeks, and cannot blush', a phrase which might have been applied to Marston. His small legs, which are called a sign

[3] Penniman, *War*, 81-4; *Poetaster* Introd., xxxviii; Baskerville *Eng. Elements in Jonson's Early Comedies*, 120-2.

of gentility, are also assigned to Crispinus; but here in *Cynthia's Revels* the scene is evidently satirizing the ladies of the court for their foolish reasons of preference.

Anaides is attended by Gelaia, laughter, the daughter of Moria, folly; Gelaia is attired as a page. He says of her (IV, iii), "I have not humoured Arete [i.e., virtue], that is held the worthiest lady in court, next to Cynthia, with half that observance and respect, as I have done her [Gelaia] in private," and he is furiously angry when he thinks her untrue. In this curious allegorical episode, Jonson seems to mean that Anaides loved to produce foolish laughter; became angry with it and scorned it when used by others, but wished to use it himself again, respecting it far more than wisdom. If Anaides were intended to be Marston, perhaps Gelaia might refer to his comedies; or the "wench in page's attire" might refer to Marston's satire, which was merely disguised sensuality. But these allegorical meanings are farfetched, and probably unnecessary. It is best taken as an example of the impudence of a certain type of courtier, giving him an opportunity for the exhibition of his foul temper.[4]

Certainly Anaides abuses Crites-Jonson, plots against him, and charges him with plagiarism, as does Crispinus. Other likenesses, to sum them up, are few. He has the name of Impudent, and a coarse and cruel humor; pride in station and rank, as Crispinus in gentility, and, as a single physical resemblance, small legs.

There is a much greater resemblance to the class of Jonson's figures represented by Tucca and especially Carlo Buffone. Here his impudence, looseness, oaths and coarseness correspond with the unblushing bravado of Tucca and Carlo. No one would think of calling Crispinus a "swaggering coachhorse," but it would fit the others. When Anaides in his anger says to Hedon, "I will garter my hose with your guts," he is talking somewhat in Marston's vein, as Penniman insists; but even more like Bobadill and his successors, Carlo and Tucca. In short, his whole tone is that belonging to this

---

[4] Baskerville says (p. 279), "Gelaia is one of the most piquant figures in the play, but I know of no similar treatment in literature." He mentions a slight resemblance to Pipenetta in Lily's Midas (p. 240). Certainly the incident does not sound like one of Jonson's own invention, and knowing his habits, one would expect a classical source.

type of the impudent, loud-mouthed, bullying jester, and is not at all that of Crispinus-Marston. It seems that he is a type-figure, perhaps with certain traits drawn directly from life, but not from either Marston or Dekker. I can find no sure reference in the entire play to either of them.

Small identified Hedon with Marston chiefly upon the evidence of the pasage in *Satiromastix*, which is very uncertain ground. He also tried unsuccessfully to identify Hedon with Crispinus. Penniman took Anaides to be Marston, from a still more unwarranted use of the *Satiromastix* passage, and because he had already wrongly identified Carlo Buffone with Marston, on the strength of a single passage.

In *Cynthia's Revels* we have Jonson writing a play primarily against the follies of courtiers. He was not writing it purposely against his detractors, as he was to do in the *Poetaster*. But having, perhaps, 'too much ego in his cosmos', he took the opportunity of showing himself, in the character of Crites, undergoing undeserved detraction. Probably his thought was that Crites was simply an emblem of virtue persecuted but finally victorious. I do not believe he identified any character with Marston. He used in the play a trifling man of pleasure, such as Fastidious Brisk had been; and a truculent, swearing, impudent man, such as Bobadill, Carlo Buffone and Tucca were. Both types of characters were elevated, however, to fit their court surroundings; instead of city-gallants or blustering sham-soldiers, he showed courtiers. He opposed to them a figure which possessed many of his own characteristics; therefore he possibly was led to give them now and then some of the general traits of his enemies. That is as much as we can affirm with tolerable certainty. That the play was chiefly satire upon the affectations of the court is evident; any element bearing upon the stage-quarrel would have to be thrust in. I do not believe it is to be found.

WHAT YOU WILL

Marston's *What You Will* must be dated between *Cynthia's Revels*, 1600-1601, to which it contains references, and the *Poetaster*, of the early summer of 1601, to which it does not allude. Oddly enough, no allusion of the *Poetaster* can be traced to *What You Will*, which seems an easy play to satirize, and which was quite plainly directed against Jonson. The first known edition of *What You Will* is that of 1607; this seems to be a revised form, since there are passages where the same character is given two names.[1] Marston may have profited by attacks in the *Poetaster* on this play, and altered it so that we have lost the clue to *Poetaster* references. This would also help to explain the fact, that of the thirty-two words and phrases cast up by Crispinus less than half have been found in Marston's works.[2]

The sources of the plot are Plautus' *Amphitruo,* and Sforza D'Oddi's *I Morti Vivi,* 1576. But the characters of Lampatho, Quadratus and Simplicius are original with Marston.

Quadratus in the general plot greatly resembles Planet in that of *Jack Drum's Entertainment;* Planet was largely representative of the author. Simultaneously Quadratus is cynic, stoic and epicurean. This appears where he is introduced, scoffing at distracted love. Like Hamlet, he says, "All that exists takes valuation from Opinion, a giddy minion." When the lover Jacomo calls on pity and piety, Quadratus pessimistically but half jocularly answers:

> "Fetch cords; he's irrecoverable; mad, rank mad.
> He calls for strange chimeras, fictions,
> That have no being . . .
> Pity and piety are long since dead . . .
> Ha! Fortune blind? away!
> How can she, hoodwinked, then so rightly see
> To starve rich worth and glut iniquity? . . .
> Love only hate; affect no higher
> Than praise of Heaven, wine, a fire."[3]

He laughs at the satirist Lampatho and his follower Simplicius as he does at Jacomo. When Lampatho threatens,

> "So Phoebus warm my brain, I'll rhyme thee dead,
> Look for the satire,"

Quadratus disdains him with mockery and then anger:

> "Rivo! St. Mark! Let's talk as light as air;
> Unwind youth's colours, display ourselves,

[1] For references, cf. Small, *Stage Quarrel,* p. 109.
[2] Cf. infra.
[3] I, i, 40f. Cf. his song near the end of II, i —

> "Music, tobacco, sack and sleep
> The tide of sorrow backward keep, etc.'

46

So that you envy-starved cur may yelp
And spend his chaps at our fantasticness . . . .
        Why, you Don Kinsader! . . .
Think'st thou a libertine, an ungyved breast,
Scorns not the shackles of thy envious clogs?
You will traduce us into public scorn?
    LAMPATHO. By this hand I will.' (II, i, 139).

Quadratus often returns to this subject — Lampatho's attempt to restrict gaiety:

"So't be fantastical 'tis wit's life-blood . . .
And I were hanged, I would be choked
Fantastically . . .
    Nay, leave protests; pluck out your snarling fangs . . .Go to,
here's my hand; and you want forty shillings, I am your Mecaenas."

In IV, i Quadratus is seen praising wine; he dips in it a
sonnet of Lampatho's, "to make it sweet".

"LAM. I'll be revenged!
QUAD. How, prithee? in a play? Come, come, be sociable."

Quadratus, then, is a mixed character. Sometimes he is
gay; sometimes, as at the end of the play, with the prince,
he is almost a malcontent. He frequently satirizes, but the
object of his attack is chiefly satire itself, as personified by
Lampatho. Most frequently he is a witty hedonist: gallant
rich, fat, a firm believer in wine, woman and song, and yet
having an undertone of sadness. Marston always depicts him
favorably. He was not putting himself on the stage in Quadratus, but I believe he was representing his feelings toward
life, as they were at that stage of his development. It was a
phase full of odd mixtures, of beginnings and endings, and
was bound to be a passing one.

Opposed to Quadratus is Lampatho; contrasted to the genial,
fantastic but clear-witted courtier-satirist is the snarling, envious scholar-satirist. It seems clear that Marston is intending to contrast the gentlemanly spirit in which he himself satirizes, to the more bitter spirit of Jonson's satire.

Simplicius, the foolish admirer of Lampatho, introduces
him:

"Do you see that gentleman? He goes but in black satin, as you
see, but, by Helicon! he hath a cloth-of-tissue wit. He breaks a jest;

47

ha, he'll rail against the court till the gallants — O God, he is very nectar." (II, i, 29).

The succeeding speech of Lampatho is probably a burlesque of Jonson's manner of speaking:

"Sir, I protest I not only take distinct notice of your dear rarities of exterior presence, but also I protest I am most vehemently enamoured, and very passionately dote on your inward adornments and habilities of spirit! I protest I shall be proud to do you most obsequious vassalage." (II, i).

Lampatho threatens Quadratus, "I'll rhyme thee dead! Look for the satire!", but Quadratus answers by calling him

"Thou canker-eaten, rusty cur! Thou snaffle to freer spirits!
. . . Shall a free-born, . . . quake at the frowns of a ragg'd satirist, a scrubbing railer?
LAM. O, sir, you are so square⁴ you scorn reproof.
QUAD. No, sir; should discreet Mastigophoros . . .",

and he proceeds to parody a speech of Crites in *Cynthia's Revels,* III, ii, which began, "If good Chrestus" etc.

During the course of the play Lampatho is gradually reformed by Quadratus. In the next scene, II, ii, he is shown as melancholy, because his scholarship has brought him so little. There is what seems to be a parody of Jonson's style:

"I relish not this mirth; my spirit is untwist;
My heart is ravelled out in discontents.
I am deep-thoughtful, and I shoot my soul
Through all creations of omnipotence."

In III, ii, Lampatho is the typical satirist:

"Dreadless of racks, strappado, or the sword . . .
I'll stand as confident as Hercules,
And with a frightful resolution,
Rip up and lance our time's impieties."

But his companions make fun of him as his wrath mounts, until he suddenly subsides, acknowledging:

⁴ Marston takes the name Quadratus from the four-square, 'entire' man of Senecan philosophy.

48

> "This is the strain that chokes the theatres;
> That makes them crack with full-stuffed audience;
> This is your only humour in request,
> Forsooth, to rail . . . This people gape for, . . .
> This admiration and applause pursues,"

but he says his humour is changed and he will rail no more.
His arrogance has so diminished, by the end of IV, i, that
when a play of his announced, and Jacomo asks, "Is't good?
Is't good?" Lampatho answers,

> "I fear 'twill hardly hit.
> QUAD. I like thy fear well; 'twill have better chance;
> There's nought more hateful than rank ignorance."

It turns out (V, i) that the play is "A comedy, entitled
Temperance", and the duke greets the name with, "The itch
on Temperance, your moral play." 'Temperance' would refer
to the moral of *Cynthia's Revels.*

Lampatho was obviously meant to bring Jonson to the mind
of the audience, and it would seem that the actor who took
the part must have impersonated Jonson. He dresses in ragged
black (the 'satin' of II, i is perhaps ironical); is a 'rusty,
fusty scholar' (IV, i) with starved ribs — a 'stiff-jointed,
tatter'd, nasty, tabor-faced[5] pedant' (II, i). Likewise
Simplicius on the stage may have been made up to suggest one
of Jonson's admirers. Lampatho is taunted with "Lamp-oil,
watch-candles, rug gowns, and small juice, thin commons,
four-o'clock rising," and with being an 'inky scholar' who
could not get into the way of the times. Simplicius says of
him, 'If you but sip of his love, you were immortal', referring
to Jonson's estimate of his own work. He is 'devote to
mouldy customs of hoar eld', that is, the classics. His absurd
compliments when he first meets Laverdure (II, i) may be
paralleled by the rebuke in *Satiromastix* to Horace, when
he is compelled to swear not to use "compliment" in the lords'
rooms after the play.

There can be no question of Marston's intent to satirize
Jonson in the person of Lampatho[6], or that we find here a

---

[5] Jonson's lack of a beard is ridiculed in *Satiromastix*. Cf. infra,
pp. 69-70.

[6] For an account of the confusion arising from "Don Kinsader" applied to Lampatho, see Appendix C.

fairly accurate if malicious portrait of Jonson. It is interesting to compare it with the other satires on Jonson, — Chrysoganus in Marston's part of *Histriomastix*, Brabant Senior in *Jack Drum*, and Horace in *Satiromastix*. Chrisoganus is much like Lampatho, in so far as they are both poor and bitter satirists. Brabant was not intended as a satire on Jonson himself, but on one of his literary methods which is not alluded to in *What You Will;* consequently there is little if any likeness. Horace is a fuller portrait, but cast in the same mould, and only altered by the necessity of adapting the Horace of the *Poetaster*.

The real purpose of *What You Will*, however, was not to attack the person of Jonson, but his last play, *Cynthia's Revels*. Jonson had made a justified attack on the extremes of court frivolity and mannerism, in a well-worked-up if somewhat cumbrous plan. Marston twisted his meaning, making it appear that Jonson was attacking freedom and jollity, or, at the worst, 'fantasticness', and wrote *What You Will* to overthrow this man of straw. There are continual allusions to the subject-matter of *Cynthia's Revels,* and at least two direct parodies[7]. It was to make this satire of the play more effective that he attacked the author as he did, asserting that he was a dull pedant, and a bitter satirist opposed to innocent merriment. To draw this character more sharply, he contrasted with it a genial, courtly satirist, who might be called Marston's ideal of a maker of satire. The relations of these two in the play is Marston's picture of the relation between himself and Jonson. It is no wonder that Jonson was furious, and broke his self-imposed and only partially preserved silence to write his answer, the *Poetaster*.

The only other personal satire in *What You Will* is that on Simplicius Faber. He is drawn at greater length in *Satiro-*

[7] One already referred to, "Should discreet Mastigophorus" etc.; cf. *supra*, p. 48. The other follows it; Quadratus says that railing is the fashion, and that a man can "scarce eat good meat, anchovies, caviare, but he's satired and termed fantastical." Mercury had said of Asotus (*Cyn. Rev.* II, i), "He doth learn to make strange sauces, to eat anchovies, maccaroni, . . . and caviare, because he loves them."

mastix as Asinius Bubo[8]. We do not know enough about Jonson's circle to hazard a guess as to the original of Simplicius, but he seems to be taken from real life. 'Faber' might just possibly indicate that the man attacked was named Smith.[9]

THE POETASTER

This is one of the greatest of English satiric plays. It was produced in the spring of 1601.[1] Whether or not Jonson had previously attacked Marston directly, here at any rate he avowedly comes out, with horse, foot and artillery, bringing up all his powerful resources for the overthrow of his younger critic. The play is conclusive evidence of the greatness of Jonson's powers; like everything he did, it is a massive piece of work, thoroughly planned and skillfully executed, each detail thought out. If any evidence were needed to show the difference between the temper of the combatants, it would be furnished by even a casual reading of this play and the *Satiromastix*. It is a fight between battleaxe, grimly wielded to kill, and wooden bludgeon, used by a smiling antagonist to give a bloody coxcomb.

[8] Here we get a hint of Marston's influence in Dekker's play. Asinius left school at "as in *praesenti*", the beginning of the conjugations in Lily's *Latin Grammar;* so did the schoolboy Holofernes in *What You Will*, II, ii, 75.

[9] There have been other attempts at identification. In the Induction are mentioned Snuff, Mew and Blirt, "three of the most-to-be feared auditors" who "sit heavy on the skirts of his scenes." Fleay indicates, with no apparent reason, Armin, Jonson and Middleton as their originals. (*Chr.* II, 77). It was half a year after that Middleton brought out his *Blurt, Master Constable*. (See Bullen's ed. of *Middleton* for evidence that the play was after Sept., 1601.) In truth, these three auditors are merely personifications of the usual means of expressing displeasure by an audience; there would be no point in bringing any real person into the Induction in such a manner as is done here.

Fleay also conjectures that Philomuse, one of the speakers of the Induction, was "Daniel, whose *Musophilus* was written in 1599". Much more probably Philomuse simply represents a friend of the poet — any admirer of his work, as the name indicates.

[1] Small, p. 203, says June; Wallace gives the date as April. The play was inspired by *What You Will*, and was written in 15 weeks, as Jonson states in the Prologue. But there is no certain date for *What You Will*, save its relations to this play.

51

Jonson himself asserts almost in so many words that this
is his first answer to the three years' assaults of his professional enemies.

> "Sure I am, three years
> They did provoke me with their petulant styles
> On every stage; and I at last, unwilling,
> But weary, I confess, of so much trouble,
> Thought I would try if shame could win upon em."[2]

It is not necessary to believe that Jonson meant that this
was the first time he had made personal allusions in his plays,
directed at his detractors. Thus he says in the Dialogue,

> "I used no names. My *books* have still been taught
> To spare the persons, and to speak the vices."

This is in answer to the allegation that he attacked

> "The law and lawyers, captains and the players
> By their particular names."

He used no names, indeed; but that was because it was
both libelous and unnecessary. No matter how many professions of superior aloofness from quarrel Ben Jonson might
make, we find it hard to believe that a man of his irascible
and eager temperament could have endured without audible
protest the slings and arrows of the satirists, 'the spitting
forth of the squeezed juice from their black jaws'. It is
possible that there are a number of personal references in his
plays which are completely lost upon modern readers.

Nevertheless, so far as we can judge now, Jonson had not
really attacked Marston at all personally on the stage, — the
naming of *Histriomastix* was as close as he had approached
to it. It is possible that Marston was able to see uncomplimentary references to himself in *Cynthia's Revels*, where
we today see nothing. At any rate, he answered with a direct

[2] *Apologetical Dialogue.* It almost seems as though Jonson wrote
the following lines of his Prologue with modern commentators of
his earlier plays in view:

> "They could wrest,
> Pervert and poison all they hear or see,
> With senseless glosses and allusions."

52

assault in *What You Will;* and then Jonson determined to
overwhelm his presumptuous foe. To find a fitting and unas-
sailable representative for himself — a great but sensitive
author attacked, from sheer malignity and perversity, by a
swarm of 'base detractors and illiterate apes' — he went on a
congenial journey to classic Rome of the Augustan age, and
chose the first great Roman satirist, Horace. By keeping
strictly to classical atmosphere, literature and history, he believed he could best shield himself from any return criticism:
Envy herself is to despair, because the scene is Rome.[3]

Marston was the principal object of assault; Dekker is
wholly secondary. It is Crispinus who is lashed; Fannius is
contemptuously laughed at. The personal satire upon Marston
begins in the second act. Crispinus is a poor relation of a lady
who is on the fringe of court, and he comes to the tradesman's
house where she has been living. He is received, after some
doubt, and wins the favour of Chloe, the tradesman's wife.
In the third act Jonson borrows from the Satires of Horace
the incident where Horace is dogged by a persistent poetaster.
In the fourth act Crispinus goes to the unfortunate banquet
where the 'younger set' at court are detected and punished by
Augustus. Crispinus and others plot to disgrace Horace and
Virgil, but in the fifth act Crispinus and Demetrius are
brought before an informal court presided over by Virgil, with
Horace as prosecutor. The poetasters are punished, Crispinus
being compelled to vomit his uncouth vocabulary. Tucca
throughout plays the part of bully, false friend and blundering
jester.

There is no doubt but that Jonson is satirizing Marston
under the name of Crispinus; but here again the critic should
beware of being carried too far in his enthusiasm for identification. Crispinus is by no means identical with Marston. There
is a large amount of personal reference, but much of it is for
us doubtful in its application, and we must be cautious in
ascribing any personal trait to Marston unless it be elsewhere
corroborated. We probably have here an unusually accurate
portrait, since the play was so direct an attack; but as with

[3] Envy's speeches rather set the tone for those of Horace's detractors later. Baskerville (p. 288) has suggested that Jonson's use
of envy is an example of the various satiric defiances to Envy or Detraction common at the time.

all these satiric characters, some of the details are those of the type, not of the individual, and others are introduced merely to help on the plot of the play. Thus, we must not suppose that Crispinus' songs are introduced to indicate that Marston was a wretched musician. A parody of bad singing could only have lasted for a few lines. Jonson was writing for a children's company, whose singing was one of their chief attractions; an important member of the cast, such as would necessarily play the part of Crispinus, would be expected to display his voice, and the play would accordingly be written to exhibit it.

Again, episodes and details that are borrowed by Jonson directly from the writings of Horace, or are naturally suggested therefrom, are clearly not personal to Marston. The third act is largely Roman, not Elizabethan. Even Crispinus' vanity, in desiring to be urged to sing, is Horatian.[4] As Marston shows his own character in his plays, we cannot imagine that he was a toady or a parasite; indeed as far as fortune went, he seems to have been Jonson's superior, and incidents such as his arrest for debts at the end of the act, and his poor costume at the beginning are only applicable to the character of Crispinus, as distinct from Crispinus the caricature of Marston. Here Jonson was striving to give the effect that, as Crispinus was to Horace, so Marston was to Jonson, and it is only in lines here and there that Marston seems to be personally referred to. We can well believe the "hot disposition naturally" to have been true of Marston. But it was enough for Jonson's purpose to represent the Roman Crispinus as mean and degraded. Thus he was first introduced as a rather negligible character; even the subservient jeweller does not pay much attention to him. Chloe suspects his gentility, and he seems more at ease with the characters of lower rank.

[4] Hor., *Lib.* I, *Sat.* ix is Jonson's main source for this third act, and here we find a hint for the song-contest of the previous act: "Invideat quod et Hermogenes ego canto." Cf. also I, ii: "Ut, quamvis tacet Hermogenes, cantor tamen atque optimus est modulator", and

"Omnibus hoc vitium est cantoribus, inter amicos
ut nunquam inducant animum cantare rogati,
iniussi numquam desistant."

It is probable that personal satire was put on the Elizabethan stage with considerable caution, much less frequently than has often been assumed by critics, who tend to find a bird or two in every bush. Many characters were undoubtedly drawn from life, as they are today on our stage; and occasionally a figure was put on that was meant to be recognized by the audience, and yet escape the charge of libel. The Register of the Privy Council on May 10, 1601, records troubles sprung from staging "the persons of some gentlemen of good desert and quality that are yet alive under obscure manner, but yet in such a sort that all the hearers may take notice both of the matter and the persons that are meant thereby."[5] This would seem to indicate that the practise was then a novel one, and was not likely to be long tolerated. There is justification for looking for hidden references to real men, but it has certainly been carried too far when almost every character in certain plays is related to the history of contemporary literature.[6]

It is not sure, though it is probable, that Crispinus would be represented on the stage as some sort of recognizable caricature of Marston's ordinary appearance. But certain points of his person and character are introduced again and again, and probably throw light on the real Marston. When Crispi-

[5] Ordish, *Early London Theatres*, p. 90; Halliwell-Phillipps, *Outlines*, 6th ed., I, p. 342; Penniman, *War*, p. 106.

[6] The identification of Horace with Jonson is even less close than that of Crispinus with Marston; e. g., Jonson at this time, player and playwright for Henslowe, and branded in 1599, was by no means a friend and frequenter of the English court, as he came to be later, and as he makes Horace in the court at Rome.

Similarly, in the case of his Virgil, Jonson did not refer to any contemporary. Was Ben Jonson the man to set up any of his fellow poets as his entire superior? Such a rank he would have allowed to none but his masters, the classic writers. The *Poetaster* furnishes a study in Roman history preparatory to *Sejanus*, to which indeed Jonson alludes at the end of the play.

Tucca was drawn from "honest Captain Hannam", as we are told in the Prologue to Satiromastix. This is all we know of him; Jonson was evidently attracted to build up a character sketch by certain odd and forceful characteristics of Hannam. (There is a Richard Hamman, the 'keeper' of the "Roaring Girl", mentioned in Bullen's *Middleton*, Vol. IV, p. 4.) That Tucca formed the bond between Crispinus and Demetrius (Dekker) is of course no more than an exigency of the plot of Jonson's play.

nus appeared in the second act, he must have formed a contrast to the brilliantly arrayed courtly assemblage. Marston's father seems to have been well-off, and it is doubtful if he were ever reduced to extreme poverty of apparel. The poor clothes which are indicated might be simply one means of degrading the character for stage appearance, and as much is implied in *Satiromastix*.[7] But it would be probable that Crispinus and Demetrius, and possibly Horace, would appear on the stage made up in such a way as would identify them to their audience. Elizabethan London was a small enough city so that established dramatists would be public characters; many of the spectators at plays must have known their authors by sight.

Two personal characteristics Jonson insists upon in his portrayal of Crispinus — red hair and little legs. It is remarkable that in several of Marston's plays he should have ridiculed red hair,[8] and one would naturally expect that he himself did not have it; but from the evidence of the *Poetaster* we must be compelled to think that he did, and that his own references were ironic — which after all would be not unlike what we know of Marston's usual vein in regard to himself.

Crispinus is made the butt of many jokes concerning his boasted gentility; the only point of this would have been Marston's own pride of ancestry, a trait which would naturally arouse the self-made Jonson's ire. The play's stress on this point suggests possible previous recriminations on the part of Marston; Jonson, in spite of his brick-making, himself claimed arms. The word "gentleman" is used of Crispinus again and again throughout the *Poetaster,* until it must have become something like a gag.[9] Much comment has been

[7] Prologue.

[8] "But, in good verity, la, he is as proper a gentleman in reversion as — and, indeed, as fine a man as may be, having a red beard and a pair of warpt legs;" *Malcontent* (1604) V, iii. "Troth, I have a good head of hair, a cheek not as yet waned, a leg, i'faith, in the full. I ha' not a red beard, take not tobacco much;" *Ant. and Mell.* III, ii. "His beard is directly brick-colour;" *What You Will,* IV, i, 31.

Crispinus is given no praenomen in Horace; perhaps Jonson's addition of 'Rufus' was suggested by the colour of Marston's hair.

[9] For example, Caesar, after the banquet, asks Crispinus who he is. He answers, "Your gentleman parcel-poet, sir;" to which Caesar answers, turning away, "O, that profaned name!"

expended upon his arms — 'Cri-spinas: a face crying in chief, and beneath a bloody toe, between three thorns pungent' — but the suggested similarity to the arms of Marston seems too far-fetched and slight to be anything more than an ingenious guess of the Fleay variety. The crude jest of the foolish interpretative picture would be all that could have been dramatically effective.[10]

The chief means of attack upon Marston and Dekker is evidently ridicule of their literary style, and especially of their vocabulary. This attack is divided into two parts: throughout the play we find Crispinus speaking in an affected way; and at the end are the parodies and penalties of the trial scene. At the first entrance of Crispinus, we find Jonson already putting into his mouth unusual and 'hard' words, and endowing him with preciosity of speech. He begins by affectedly saying, "You are most delicately seated here, full of sweet delight and blandishment." He is "most strenuously well"; he "vehemently desires to participate in the knowledge of her fair features"; farther on: "Let it suffice, I must relinquish, and so, in a word" (thus calling attention to the inflated phraseology), "please you to expiate this compliment." The use of the word "sweet" at the beginning of the third act is noticeable; it is repeated six times on the first two pages. At one time it seems to have been a favorite of Marston, especially in his *Antonio and Mellida*. When Crispinus is seized by bailiffs he exclaims magniloquently, "Seek not to eclipse my reputation thus vulgarly. . . Nay, I beseech you, gentlemen, do not exhale me thus, remember 'twas but

[10] Heraldry was rapidly running to seed in Elizabethan times, and these word-pictures were very common among the newer nobility. Jonson had utilized them before in his treatment of Sogliardo. Dr. Nicholson (Grosart's ed., *Marston's Poems*) suggests that Jonson in the 'bloody toe between three thorns' may have had reference to Marston's true arms, which included a fess dancetée (Horizontal band across the middle of the shield, indented) between three fleur-de-lis. Grosart disbelieves the suggestion; Mallory adopts it. The special mark (difference) of Marston's particular branch of the family was a crescent in one upper corner — hence the "crying face in chief". But this connection seems fanciful.

Fleay's idea that a play upon the word 'Marston' was meant — 'mars' and the obsolete plural 'toen', seems far-fetched, especially since, as Small pointed out, only one toe was represented.

for sweetmeats. I am forfeited to eternal disgrace, if you do not commiserate. Good officer, be not so officious." Little of this affected language sounds to a reader's ear particularly Marstonian — the extremes of that style are unmistakeable, and they are not found here. That Jonson could catch his literary style is more than sufficiently proved in the last act; and this forcing of Crispinus' language would lose most of its point if it were not aimed at Marston. It is possible that Marston's talk had contracted the fashion of the day, and was here ridiculed as Hamlet ridiculed Osric, whose tongue was affected by the same disease.

We can better appreciate the assault on Marston's style which concludes the play. The verses which are acknowledged by Crispinus as his own work, form a clever and just parody, and the passage is worth quoting in full because it exposes so completely Marston's two worst faults of style — turbid thought and turgid vocabulary:

"Ramp up, my genius, be not retrograde,
But boldly nominate a spade a spade.
What, shall thy lubrical and glibbery Muse
Live, as she were defunct, like punk in stews?"

(The licentious Tucca interpollates, "Excellent!")

"Alas, that were no modern consequence,
To have cothurnal buskins frighted hence.
No, teach thy incubus to poetize
And throw abroad thy furious snotteries,
Upon that pufft-up lump of barmy froth . . .
Or clumsy chillblained judgment; that, with oath,
Magnificates his merit, and bespawles
The conscious time with humorous foam, and brawls
As if his organons of sense would crack
The sinews of my patience. Break his back,
O poets all, and some: For now we list
Of strenuous venge-ance to clutch the fist.
                    Subscri. Cris.

TUCCA. Aye marry, this was written like a Hercules in poetry now."

That this is fair parody is evident, when such passages as the following, from the beginning of the *Scourge of Villainy*, can be found not infrequently in the early work of Marston:

58

"Black cypress crown me, whilst I up do plough
The hidden entrails of rank villainy,
Tearing the veil from damn'd impiety.
Quake, guzzle dogs, that live on putrid slime,
Skud from the lashes of my yerking rhyme." [11]

Most of the words or phrases Jonson ascribes to Crispinus
can be found in Marston's work, and there are numerous
reasons to account for those that cannot. It was an imitation
of style as well as vocabulary, and would include odd words
because they were odd and of the same general kind that
Marston used. Small conjectured that in Marston's alteration of *What You Will* he may have omitted words which
Jonson had derided. Certainly we do not find most of them
in Marston's later work.[12]

Verses confessed by Demetrius follow, in sing-song measure,
as contrast. No satire on Dekker's vocabulary is intended,
but merely on his general style, with its rather slipshod manner
and loose thought.

The farcial ending of the purge was borrowed from Lucian,
as the *Satiromastix* noted in its Prologue;[13] it must have been

[11] Or compai. the beginning of the sixth satire of the *S. V.*
[12] A few notes on individual words, supplementary to the work of
Mallory and Penniman, follow. *Lubrical* has not been found in
Marston, but it is exactly the kind of word he would be expected to
use (cf. the frequent appearances of *glibbery, slippery, lewd, snot-
tery,* etc.). *Modern* is defined for this place in Mallory's glossary as
'trivial, trifling'; but it would seem to have the other, regular meaning, 'of the time, fashionable', which is also used in the *Poetaster,*
III, iv, 332. Cf. *A. M.,* Ind.: "acting a modern braggadoch." *Incubus* is found in *A. R.* IV, ii. 21, and I, i, 1: "If the incubus that
rides your bosom would have patience." *Poetize* may be meant to
ridicule the formation of verbs by adding this ending, as in Clove's
use in *Ev. Man Out,* III, i: *modelizing, diamondizing. Magnificates
his merit* is plainly borrowed from the *S. V.,* Lib. II, Proem.: "I cannot with swol'n lines magnificate mine own poor worth". It also
may have reference to the poetaster's anger against the close of
Cynthia's Revels, "By—'tis good, and if you like't you may."
Humourous foam of course refers. to Jonson's Humour plays; I do
not recall a use of the word *foam* in Marston, though *froth* is common. *Of strenuous venge-ance to clutch the fist* is taken from *Antonio's Revenge,* V. i: "The fist of strenuous vengeance is clutched."
But Marston seems generally to have used it as two syllables. *A. M.,*
III, ii, 261; IV, i, 115; *S. V.,* XI, 153.
[13] For similar earlier examples on the English stage, see Baskerville,
pp. 44, and 307, note 2.

59

one of the best-acting scenes of the *Poetaster*. That it was not without effect we can see from the chastened vocabulary of Marston's subsequent plays. As 'Horace' said, the pills "were somewhat bitter, sir, but wholesome." [14]

It must be remembered that the *Poetaster* had a wider design than a simple attack upon Marston. It was the one most important statement of Jonson's case in his long quarrel with his surroundings. According to his belief, his was a case of greatness not only unrecognized, but slandered. The trial scene displays Jonson's attitude most forcefully. After praising himself under the name of Horace, he set out his grievances in the shape of a formal indictment,[15] which sums up the scattered attacks in the rest of the play:

[14] Cf. supra, p. 49. There are 29 words, as distinguished from peculiar phrases, given in the qto. Of these words, 13 are now to be found in the writings of Marston, and 9 of these are still in use. It may be noticed that the words occur roughly in groups, first from *S. V.*:(*glibbery*, common; *magnificate*, Proem. II; *snotteries*, II, 71); then from *Jack Drum*: (*chilblained*, II, 136; *clumsy*, ib; *barmy*, I, 35; *froth*, ib.); then seven in succession which are not to be found in Marston (*inflate, turgidous, ventosity*, with which cf. Clove in *Every Man Out*, III, i; *oblatrant, obcaecate, furibund, fatuate*). Then follows *strenuous*, not uncommon in Marston, and *conscious*, the only one of the words to be found in our version of *W. Y. W.* (III, iii, 25). From *Antonio's Revenge* come *damp* (I, ii, 140) *clutched*, (I, i, etc), and *snarling gusts* (prol.). The list is concluded with five words not found in Marston, *obstupefact, tropological, anagogical, loquacity, pinnosity*. The last four, together with *obcaecate*, are omitted from the folio. It may well be that these four words, different in quality from the rest, were added by the actors, and excised by Jonson from his carefully edited quarto. From the grouping given above, it may be surmised that the seven words not found in Marston, but sounding like words of his choice — the words beginning with *inflate* — may have occurred in the first version of *W. Y. W.*, especially as *conscious*, just after, is still to be found there. These vomited words would be very likely to be remembered by audiences, and what more likely than that Marston should have changed them in his play of about the same time, if only to avoid unpleasant reminiscent laughter?

Retrograde was used in *Cyn. Rev.* V, iii, 4, in affected language. *Reciprocal*, Penniman says (*Poet.* p. 256) is not found in Marston, though he had given the reference *Mal.* II, ii, 62 in his *War*, p. 118. *Prorumpt* is not found; Jonson may well have used it only for its excellent onamatopoeic effect.

[15] The indictment is drawn up in the same form as one in the second act of *A Warning for Fair Women*, printed 1599. Both are presumably drawn from regular law-forms.

60

HORACE. I am the worst accuser under heaven . . .
I take no knowledge that they do malign me.
TIB. Aye, but the world takes knowledge.
HOR. Would the world knew
How heartily I wish a fool should hate me."

The indictment is against

"Rufus Laberius Crispinus, alias Crispinas, Poetaster and Plagiary;
the other, by the name of Demetrius Fannius, playdresser and plagiary;
that you (not having the fear of Phoebus, or his shafts, before your
eyes) . . . have most ignorantly, foolishly, and (more like yourselves)
maliciously, gone about to deprave, and calumniate the person and
writings of Quintus Horatius Flaccus, here present, Poet, and priest
to the Muses: and to that end have mutually conspired and plotted
. . . for the better accomplishing your base and envious purpose;
taxing him, falsely, of self-love, arrogancy, impudence, railing, filching
by translation, etc."

So far as we can judge today, their taxing had on the con-
trary not been false; precisely these characteristics were true
of Jonson to a very high degree. Even impudence was his,
when he could call Marston and Dekker poetaster and playdresser, and himself "Poet, and priest to the Muses." That
he was much the greater poet is true, but his arrogance was
excessive.

There follow the parodies of the poetasters' verse, after
which Horace defends himself:

"When hast thou known us wrong, or tax a friend?
I dare thy malice to betray it . . .
Rather such speckled creatures as thyself,
Should be eschewed and shunned: such as will bite
And gnaw their absent friends, not cure their fame . . ."

This retort[16] simply turns back upon them the character that
Marston had given Lampatho-Jonson in *What You Will*.
Horace goes on to say that they "devise things never seen or
heard, t'impair men's names." This may be an allusion
to characters such as Lampatho or Brabant Senior, which,
while they do contain hits at Jonson, are not intended to be
actual portraits of him — though he may well have taken them
for such.

[16] Taken from Horace's *Satires*, I, iv, 78-85.

Jonson's Virgil sums up the trial:

"Where there is true and perfect merit,
There can be no dejection . . .
Here-hence it comes, our Horace now stands taxed
With impudence self-love and arrogance,
By these, who share no merit in themselves,
And therefore think, his portion is as small.
For they, from their own guilt, assure their souls,
If they should confidently praise their works,
In them it would appear inflation, —
Which, in a full and well-digested man,
Cannot receive that foul abusive name,
But the fair title of erection . . ."[17]
Now, Romans, you have heard our thoughts. Withdraw, when you
please."

This passage, of which I have quoted only a part, is his real
defence against all his adversaries, and the conclusion was
written in much the same vein as the famous ending of
Cynthia's Revels, "By — 'tis good, and if you like't, you may."
Undoubtedly Jonson had enough strength in satire 'for anything', but he spoils the whole effect of what he says so well,
by evincing extreme arrogance even while he is engaged in
denying that he has it. The half-playful retorts of the
'poetasters' in *Jack Drum* and *What You Will* and *Satiromastix,* are smaller projectiles propelled with much less force,
but they do more effective execution because they do not
explode of themselves before reaching the mark, as does the
Poetaster.

[17] Or, as he says in the Prologue, "a well-erected confidence". Virgil
goes on to defend translation (which they had not attacked in itself,
but in his extreme use of it — where else could scenes be found like
Poet. III, i or III, v?) and then excuses the author's "sharpness in this
play," which he calmly says "was forced out of a suffering virtue." He
ends with superb pride:

"This, like Jove's thunder, shall their pride control:
'The honest Satire hath the happiest soul'.
Now, Romans, etc."
The play concludes with the effective little song:
"Blush, folly, blush, here's none that fears
The wagging of an ass's ears,
Although a wolvish case he wears.
Detraction is but baseness' varlet;
And apes are apes, though clothed in scarlet."

The difference in Jonson's attitudes toward Marston and Dekker is interesting. Even when Jonson is flaying the former most angrily, he still seems to have some respect for him as an adversary; but Jonson affects to feel only contempt and pity for Dekker, treating him as though almost beneath notice. Probably this was to serve two purposes. Jonson would really feel some such contempt for the facile turning-off of plays by the Henslowe hack-of-all-work; certainly Dekker's reply, *Satiromastix*, if judged simply as a play must have justified Jonson's attitude as an artist. On the other hand, Dekker appears to have been an amiable man, one against whom Jonson had felt little personal offence. By putting Demetrius, as he did, into an entirely secondary, subservient place, Jonson could satisfy his contempt for the lack of care and substance in Dekker's work, and yet not press too fiercely upon him.[18] The introduction is a key to the way in which he is treated:

TUCCA (to Actor). My Poetaster [i. e., Crispinus] shall make thee a play . . .
What's he with the half-arms there, that salutes us out of his cloak like a motion, ha?
HISTRIO. O, sir, his doublet's a little decayed; he is otherwise a very simple honest fellow, sir, one Demetrius, a dresser[19] of plays about the town here; we have hired him to abuse Horace, and bring him in a play, with all his gallants." [20]

So Demetrius ends IV, i by saying,

"I'll go write, sir.
TUCCA. Do, do; stay, here's a drachm to purchase gingerbread for thy muse."

All of Jonson's wrath is saved to pour upon the head of Marston, but his contempt of Dekker must have been most galling. One is surprized that the *Satiromastix* is for the most part so light in tone.

[18] Or possibly Penniman is right in guessing that Jonson did not think of Dekker until the *Poetaster* was practically finished, and then inserted a few lines in III, iv and V, iii (*Poet*. p. lx).
[19] This word is used several times in the play; perhaps a pun on 'Dekker' is intended.
[20] *Poet*. III, i. The last phrase would imply that some of Jonson's friends were satirized in some of the minor characters of *Satiromastix;* but this vague hint is the only one we have.

It is probable, from the somewhat vague references to conspiracy in the *Poetaster,* that Jonson was rather in the dark concerning the plot which he claimed was made against him. His idea seems to have been that the players, for gain, united in furthering the personal spite of Marston; between them they hired Dekker to attack Jonson in a play, which was being written at the time the *Poetaster* was composing. In III, i the actors have hired Demetrius to abuse Horace in a play, for the reason that "it will get us a huge deal of money, captain, and we have need on't; for this winter has made us all poor as starved snakes, nobody comes at us." In IV, i Tucca says Demetrius will get a new suit for his share of the work; so "sting him, my little neufts; . . . we'll all hang upon him like so many horseleeches, the players and all."

Jonson thus assumes that the hard winter of 1600-1 was, in addition to 'envy, malice and hypocrisy', the real occasion of the plays written against him. Tucca has alluded, a little before, to the stage-quarrel; he did not wish to go to the theatre: "I would fain come with my cockatrice some day and see a play, if I knew when there was a good bawdy one; but they say you have nothing but Humours, Revels and Satires, that gird and f—t at the time, you slave." So Rosencrantz says, "Faith, there hath been much to-do on both sides, and the nation holds it no sin to tarre them to controversy; there was, for a while, no money bid for argument, unless the poet and the player went to cuffs in the question." [21] That this hard winter had much to do with encouraging the stage-presentation of the quarrel there can be no doubt. Though the seeds of enmity seem to have been sown some time before, it is doubtful if *Poetaster* and *Satiromastix* could have been produced unless personalities were required to drum up trade. It is this fact which lends an air of falsity to much of the famous 'War of the Theatres' — it is impossible to say how much of the "throwing about of brains" was inspired by real anger, and how much by the necessity of stimulating public

[21] Hamlet, II, ll. This speech probably refers to the winter of 1600-1. Even if it should refer to the next winter, however, it would make little difference; conditions were about the same, and the Children of the Chapel still under special patronage. Cf. Lee's *Shakespeare* p. 357, n. 3. Wallace (*Children of Chapel,* Ch. XIV; p. 164, believes this passage to have been written late in 1601.

curiosity. It seems natural that Jonson should have been the storm center, from his personal disposition, his popularity as a dramatist, and his connection with the children's stage which was just then impoverishing the adult companies. So we see that Kemp is apparently made to voice the feeling of his company against Jonson: "Why, here's our fellow Shakespeare puts them [i. e., university pens] all down, aye, and Ben Jonson[22] too. O that Ben Jonson is a pestilent fellow, he brought up Horace giving the poets a pill, but our fellow Shakespeare hath given him a purge that made him bewray his credit." [23]

We have watched Marston in his plays become more and more personal in his assaults on Jonson, warned only by a growl or two — the suggestion of an attack here and there in *Every Man Out* and *Cynthia's Revels*. Now for the first time we see Jonson turning upon his antagonist, with the purpose of rending his literary reputation limb from limb, and so getting rid once for all of the nuisance. There is no more doubt, no elaborate proof required, that it is Marston who is attacked; and when we compare the *supposed* satires of Marston under the names of Carlo and of Hedon or Anaides, we see how little real ground there is for believing that anything more than the threat of an attack is to be found in them. Carlo and Anaides were intended to represent types, with any personal element purposely made vague; Jonson may have had Marston sometimes in mind in details now and then, but not in his general scheme. Here he directs the whole play against Marston — the treatment of Dekker is strictly subordinated. There is intended to be no mistake that Marston is the individual meant, both in a personal and a literary way.

In the *Apologetical Dialogue,* written some time, perhaps a year, after the *Poetaster,* Jonson said,

[22] Kemp is speaking for actors and the ordinary playwrights, as opposed to learned writers such as Jonson. There has been a difference of opinion whether Ben Jonson here be subject or object; the latter is the case.

[23] *Return from Parnassus,* Two; IV, iii. (The scene is numbered in the original edition iv, through a misprint.) January 1, 1601-2. The university writer was being ironic here in his praise of Shakespeare, but the passage shows well enough the hostility between Jonson and the players.

"I can profess, I never writ that piece
More innocent, or empty of offence.
Some salt it had, but neither tooth nor gall . . .
POL. No? Why, they say you taxed
The Law, and Lawyers; Captains; and the Players,
By their particular names.
AUTHOR. It is not so.
I used no name. My books have still been taught
To spare the persons, and to speak the vices."

This I believe was in the main true of his earlier plays, but it was not true of the *Poetaster*. The very vividness of its portraiture supports Jonson's disavowal of personalities in earlier plays. Had he meant *Every Man Out* or *Cynthia's Revels* to contain a Marston character, in all probability it would have been as clear.

SATIROMASTIX

The *Poetaster* was not answered by Marston in person, but by Dekker in *Satiromastix*, which only concerns us so far as it was inspired by Marston or as it illuminates his share in the quarrel. The most probable date for the production of *Satiromastix* seems to be the summer of 1601,[1] soon after the staging of *Poetaster*.

It is hard to say how much Marston had to do with the conception of the play. Jonson says that Marston hired Dekker — and Dekker was certainly for hire. Furthermore, we know of no attack of Jonson on Dekker previous to the *Poetaster*. The satire is much more forceful that anything else of the kind in Dekker's works, but it is written by him, and there is almost no definite trace of Marston's easily distinguished style. Yet in Jonson's prefatory address, *To the World*, and in Tucca's *Epilogue*, *poetasters*, in the plural, are spoken of as having "untrussed Horace". While there is no good reason for doubting that the hand, throughout, is the hand of Dekker,

---

[1] *Cynthia's Revels* can be dated in the spring of 1601. Then Jonson began the *Poetaster*, which took fifteen weeks to write. The *Satiromastix* must have appeared soon after the *Poetaster*, while interest in the case was at its height; it was entered in the Stationers' Register November 11, 1601. It is doubtful if it would have been registered until its first novelty had been worn off; consequently it seems safe to place it in the summer of 1601.

nevertheless there seem to be two distinct tones used in the passages of attack on Jonson. One is the rather coarse but not very bitter personal abuse, which I take to be Dekker's. But here and there throughout the play there crops up an underlying tone of almost friendly and certainly respectful admonishment. This I take to be directly inspired by Marston. The praise in the Dedication to the *Malcontent* was no hypocrisy, but a true expression of Marston's feeling towards Jonson, though the two characters were so contrasted and so often at odds. The very number of persons and incidents in Marston's plays which have reference to Jonson, shows Marston realized that Jonson's work was worth repeated criticism.

Altogether, Marston must have been the originator of a reply to *Cynthia's Revels,* but entrusted its accomplishment to Dekker, perhaps from personal fear of Jonson. Jonson evidently learned of the design soon after its inception, and hastened to forestall it by his *Poetaster.* It would appear that when the other playwrights discovered this intention of Jonson's they delayed their play until the *Poetaster* appeared. Certainly Dekker could have beaten Jonson at a game of speed, had he been so minded, especially as he had the start. Possibly in the interval Dekker took a simple plot, that of William Rufus and Terril, with the design of weaving into it an answer to Jonson's play after that should have appeared. The result, when it was discovered that Augustan Rome had to be inserted into Norman England, was the singularly incongruous mixture of *Satiromastix.* Tucca's part could not have been written until after the appearance of Jonson's Tucca, and most of the abuse of Horace is put into Tucca's mouth in *Satiromastix,* and is in his peculiar vein, which Jonson originated. Similarly the entire satiric element of the play is dependent on the *Poetaster.* Jonson was simply repaid in his own coin; it is another instance of lions beginning to sculpture hunting-scenes.

Satiromastix is not such an unutterably bad play as most critics have stated. The modern eye is immediately caught by the anachronism of Horace in King William Rufus' court. To Englishmen of Elizabeth's day, who habitually saw figures from all eras of history on the stage in the latest fashion of hose and doublet, it did not seem so impossible. It is to be further remembered that this was not designed to be a serious play; the original tragi-comedy was nearly swamped in the farce relating to the stage-quarrel. The main plot of William Rufus, Sir Walter Terril and Cælestine is not badly written, and is well on a level with Dekker's other plays. This extremely simple plot is elaborated by a subplot of humours. Then evidently into this unfinished play was thrust a mass of material satirizing Horace. The result must have been somewhat equivalent to the modern light comedy with plenty of topical hits. It was certainly not intended to be seriously taken. Too many modern critics have neglected the motto from Martial which proceeds it. — detractors will be able to say nothing worse of the frivolous trifle *(Nugas)* than the author himself had said. As a work of serious literature of course it would have no standing, but that is just what the author did not mean it to be. For what he did mean it, a continuation of the quarrel, in a half-serious vein, and with much less of the deadly but self-defeating sincerity of the *Poetaster,* it succeeded excellently well.

To it was awarded the popular verdict in a much larger degree than to the *Poetaster,* much greater work as that undoubtedly is. Jonson had to confess, in his *Address to the Reader,* that he had by his play only aroused more and stronger enemies:

> "I hoped at last they would sit down and blush,
> But nothing could I find more contrary.
> And though the impudence of flies be great,
> Yet this hath so provoked the angry wasps . . .
> That they fly buzzing, mad, about my nostrils."

Not only had it not silenced his enemies, but the popular judgment had undoubtedly gone against him. So, like a true artist, he damns the crowd in good poetry:

> "But, that these beggarly and base conceits
> Should carry it, by the multitude of voices,
> Against the most abstracted work, opposed
> To the stuffed nostrils of the drunken rout,
> O, this would make a learn'd and liberal soul
> To rive his stained quill up to the back,
> And damn his long-watch'd labours to the fire,
> Things that were born when none but the still night
> And his dumb candle saw his pinching throes, —
> Were not his own free merit a more crown
> Unto his travails, than their reeling claps."

Thus his conceit saves him from too much punishment; to himself he can still be the great man holding his enemies at the mercy of his pen, if he care to use it in writing satires or public prints, though they, "like so many screaming grasshoppers held by the wings, fill every ear with noise."

Jonson's very gifts defeated themselves when employed upon drama as he chose to write it. That he had wonderful power in psychologic character-portrayal can not be doubted. That he could put it successfully into popular form is evident from his additions to the *Spanish Tragedy*. He was primarily, however, a scholar; he combined both mastery of detail and great constructional ability. But he seems to have almost entirely lacked the ability to portray, perhaps to feel, the tenderer, more romantic emotions. He was essentially intellectual, and his attempts to depict passion, such as the Ovid-Julia parting scene, are machine-made, rather than natural expressions of his own "emotions recollected in tranquillity." The age was a romantic one, and cared little for scholarship on the stage; so it is no wonder that Jonson's dramas, great as they are from the standpoint of literature, should have been something like failures in his own time. Dekker, on the other hand, was obviously unhampered by any conscientious theories of art, and knew from long apprenticeship just how to catch the popular ear. Moreover, he did not have to sustain the impossible burden of proving himself by argument and invective the greatest poet of the age.

The *Satiromastix* tells us very little about Crispinus, but a great deal about Horace. Some of this personal information about Jonson we know of in no other way, but it is probably true to fact, if not always to implication. As usual, his rugged personality dominates the scene. His personal appearance is referred to again and again: He is "thin-bearded";[2] Tucca calls him "great Hunks", and says he has a tanned skin;[3] He is "hungry-faced,[4] "as hard-favoured a fellow as your majesty has seen in a summer's day".[5] "Thou has such a villainous broad back that I warrant thou art able

[2] I, ii, 344.
[3] *Ibid.*, 1. 387.
[4] *Ibid.* 1. 455.
[5] II, i, 151.

to bear away any man's jests in England";[6] he walks "so
stately";[7] he has "the most ungodly face, by my fan; it looks,
for all the word, like a rotten russet apple when 'tis bruised.
'Tis better than a spoonful of cinnamon water next my heart,
for me to hear him speak, he sounds it so in the nose, and
talks and rants for all the world like the poor fellow under
Ludgate. . . It's cake and puddings to me to see his face
make faces when he reads his songs and sonnets." Tucca
brings on the stage a picture of Horace and a caricature of
Jonson, and compares them:

> "Thou hast such a terrible mouth, that thy beard's afraid to peep out;
> but look here, you staring Leviathan . . . Parboiled face, look:
> Horace had a trim long beard, and a reasonable good face for a poet
> (as faces go nowadays) . . . No, Horace had not his face punched
> full of eyelet holes, like the cover of a warming-pan . . Horace
> was a goodly corpulent gentleman, and not so lean a hollowcheèkt
> scrag as thou art."[8]

Jonson's clothes are mentioned in the usual terms: he
"walks in rug"[9] and thanks God he never fell into the hands
of satin;[10] Tucca calls him "Apollo's frieze-gown watchman".[11]
There are a number of gibes at his past life. "Thou writ'st
in a most goodly big hand, too — I like that — and read'st as
legibly as some that have been saved by their neck-verse".[12]
The poetasters "swear they'll bring your life and death upon'th
stage like a bricklayer in a play".[13] There are some interesting details of Jonson's unsuccessful career as an actor, concerning which we know nothing save what we learn here,
which is probably true.

> "TUCCA. Thou hast been at Paris Garden, hast not?
> HORACE. Yes, Captain, I ha' played Zulziman there . . .
> TUC. Thou call'st Demetrius journeyman poet, but thou putst up
> a supplication to be a poor journeyman player, and hadst been still so,
> but that thou couldst not set a good face upon't; thou hast forgòt how

[6] II, ii, 5.
[7] III, i, 77.
[8] V, ii.
[9] I, ii, 335.
[10] Ibid, 1. 412.
[11] IV, ii, 1.
[12] I, ii, 140.
[13] Ibid, 1. 172.

thou amblest, in leather pilch, by a playwagon, in the highway, and tookst mad Jeronimo's part, to get service among the mimics; and when the Stagerites banished thee into the Isle of Dogs, thou turnst bandog . . . and ever since bitest; . . . read, lege, save thyself and read." [14]

There is one possible reference to the fact that Jonson was the writer for the favoured Children of the Chapel at Black-friars, — Sir Vaughan's "Hold, silence, the puppet-teacher speaks!" [15]

In such references as these [16] one detects more vividness and closeness to reality than in Jonson's allegory of Crispinus, strong as that is. Surely here Jonson was repaid for whatever personal abuse he bestowed upon the poetasters.

On the literary side of the quarrel the difference from the *Poetaster's* tone is noticeable, and here it is one detects Marston's personal attitude. In the Address to the World prefixed to *Satiromastix,* "that terrible Poetomachia lately commenced" is spoken of. This supports the view that the stage quarrel was not primarily an affair of personalities, did not really have the desire to injure, until the publication of the *Poetaster.* Before that it had been partly a conflict of dramatic theories, and partly of the theatres themselves, adult companies resenting the children's successes. Jonson had received criticism on himself as dramatist with ill-concealed dislike, ever since Marston had begun to praise him in dubious terms in *Histrio-mastix,* and had continued to criticise his methods in *Jack Drum's Entertainment* and *What You Will. What You Will* proved too much for Jonson's patience; not only was the play as a whole designed as an attack upon *Cynthia's Revels,* but it contained the obvious personal picture of Lampatho. The strained theatrical condition of the time enabled Jonson to burst out into the vitriolic abuse of the *Poetaster,* which in its turn was answered in *Satiromastix.* In this way Dekker is right in saying that the real Poetomachia had only recently

[14] IV, i, 151f.

[15] IV, iii, 215.

[16] It seems odd that no mention is made of his branded thumb, in any of the satires upon Jonson, especially in this play, where several other incidents of the duel are brought up. Doubts have been expressed as to whether Jonson's sentence were ever carried out. See *Athenæum,* Mar. 6, 1886, p. 337 and June 19, p. 823.

commenced, as he is right in a measure when he goes on to
add that "it would be found on the Poetasters' side, *se
defendendo.*" Marston's criticisms were, I believe, well
meant, but they had contained too much personal ridicule.
Nevertheless it was Jonson who began the real contest, if we
can judge from what remains written of the controversy. So
Crispinus says:

> "We come like your physicians, to purge
> Your sick and dangerous mind in her disease.
> DEM. In troth we do, out of our loves we come,
> And not revenge; but, if you strike us still,
> We must defend our reputations;
> Our pens shall like our swords be always sheathed,
> Unless too much provoked." [17]

But Jonson would not be likely to appreciate the kindliness
which made the poetasters assert that they were not his
enemies, only physicians for his sick mind.

Indirectly they acknowledge the truth of some of Jonson's
statements concerning them; they do not reproach him for
untruthfulness, but for betrayal of friendship. He has mis-
used the opportunities for observation which their intimacy
had afforded:

> "But when your dastard wit will strike at men
> In corners, and in riddles fold the vices
> Of your best friends, you must not take to heart
> If they take all the gilding from their pills,
> And only offer you the bitter core . . .
> Say that you have not sworn unto your paper
> To blot her white cheeks with the dregs and bottom
> Of your friends' private vices . . .
> Say you swear . . .
> That when your lashing jests make all men bleed,
> Yet you whip none. Court, city, country, friends,
> Foes, — all must smart alike."

This confirms what would have been believed from the character of the man; as Drummond later told of him, he says
truth but cares not for injuring friends.

Jonson had rated Demetrius-Dekker below Crispinus-Marston. That his estimate of the relative rank of the two men

[17] I, ii, 294.

72

was correct is shown by the fact that *Satiromastix* continues it:

"TUCCA (to Horace). Thou wrongest here a good, honest rascal, Crispinus, and a poor varlet Demetrius Fannius (brethren in thine own trade of poetry); thou sayest Crispinus' satin doublet is raveled out here, and that this penurious sneaker is out at elbows . . . Crispinus shall give thee an old cast satin suit, and Demetrius shall write thee a scene or two, in one of thy strong garlic comedies; and thou shalt take the guilt of conscience for it, and swear 'tis thine own, old lad, 'tis thine own."[18]

The heart of the poetasters' complaint against Jonson is contained in the following serious lines, well-intentioned if sometimes not very clear. I believe Marston inspired them.[19] Horace has been made to repeat one of his avowed reasons for writing the *Poetaster*.

> "What could I do, out of a just revenge,
> But bring them to the stage? they envy me
> Because I hold more worthy company.
> DEM. Good Horace, no; my cheeks do blush for thine,
> As often as thou speakest so. Where one true
> And nobly-virtuous spirit, for thy best part
> Loves thee, I wish one ten, even from my heart.
> I make account I put up as deep share
> In any good man's love, which thy worth earns,
> As thou thyself. We envy not to see
> Thy friends with bays to crown thy poesy.
> No, here the gall lies, that we[20] know what stuff
> Thy very heart is made of, know the stalk
> On which thy learning grows, and can give life
> To thy (once dying) baseness, yet must we
> Dance antics on thy paper.
> HOR. Fannius —
> CRIS. This makes us angry, but not envious.
> No, were thy warpt soul put in a new mould,
> I'd wear thee as a jewel set in gold."[21]

This seems to have been written personally and in sincerity, almost in praise. It again states the real reason of the quarrel,

[18] I, ii, 392.
[19] Compare quotations on p. 78.
[20] So I substitute, for the sake of clearer reading, for the original *"we that"*.
[21] IV, iii, 260-278.

as the poetasters saw it; for their criticism he had retaliated by wounding wouldbe friends.

A passage such as this helps to show why the *Poetaster* was not at the time effective as an attack. As Chesterton says in his essay on *Pope and the Art of Satire*, unmixed invective is not good satire, because it is felt to be false: "It is impossible to satirize a man without having a full account of his virtues." Jonson was not generous enough to write really great satire, because he attempted to overwhelm his adversaries "with an infinite number of furious epithets." The higher kind of satire emphasizes the enemy's merits, for the sake of contrast, and in order to show that he is unworthy of possessing them. —

> "But were there one whose fires
> True genius kindles, and fair fame inspires, . . .
> Should such a man —"

It was this kind of large-mindedness which Jonson lacked, and which made his satire, cruel as was its intent, overreach itself. On the other hand the 'poetasters' show in such passages that this quality was what they did possess, and this goes far to retrieve their deficiencies of genius.

Jonson's only answer to the *Satiromastix* was his *Apologetical Dialogue*, added to the *Poetaster* some time after the appearance of Dekker's play. He defends and praises himself, as being unhurt by spite. If their attack gave them a livelihood, he says, he is glad, except that "some better natures" had been drawn into the ranks of his adversaries. He will not answer the *Satiromastix*, though he could with his satire disgrace them forever. He defends his railing by classical examples. At the end he announces he will next try tragedy, referring to *Sejanus*. To this *Sejanus* Marston was to supply complimentary verses!

The only other references of Jonson to Marston are what he said to Drummond of Hawthornden in 1616, and one of his posthumously published *Epigrams*, No. 68:

> "*Playwright*, convict of public wrongs to men,
> Takes private beatings and begins again;
> Two kinds of valour he doth show at once:
> Active in's brains, and passive in his bones."

There are a few other epigrams in the collection addressed to *"Playwright"*, most of which are quite indefinite in content.[22]

Toward the end of 1601 Marston in *Antonio and Mellida* parodied a passage of Jonson's additions to the *Spanish Tragedy*.[23] In addition to this, there is probably another fling at Jonson. We have noted that the Epilogue to Cynthia's *Revels* ended in a defiant assertion of the play's merit:

"By — 'tis good, and if you like't you may."

The Epilogue to *Antonio and Mellida* is spoken by Andrugio, still clad in the armor he wore in the last scene. It begins:

"Gentlemen, though I remain an armed Epilogue, I stand not as a peremptory challenger of desert, either for him that composed the Comedy, or for us that acted it; but a most submissive suppliant for both."

It is impossible to date this epilogue of Marston's exactly. *Antonio and Mellida* was produced some time before February-March, 1600 (N. S.), and the Epilogue might have been written at any time from then until the play was printed sometime in 1602. I believe it followed *Cynthia's Revels*, and preceded the Prologue to the *Poetaster*, which was written about June, 1601. The following passage of the *Poetaster* Prologue I believe clearly refers to the *Antonio and Mellida* armed Epilogue:

"*Enter Prologue hastily, in armour . . .*
If any muse why I salute the stage,
An armed Prologue, know, 'tis a dangerous age.
Wherein who writes, had need present his scenes
Forty-fold proof against the conjuring means
Of base detractors and illiterate apes . . .
'Gainst these, have we put on this forced defense
Whereof the allegory and hid sense
Is, that a well-erected confidence
Can fright their pride, and laugh their folly hence.
Here now, put case our author should, once more,
Swear that his play were good, he doth implore
You would not argue him of arrogance,
Howe'er that common spawn of ignorance,
Our fry of writers, may beslime his name . . ."

[22] *Epigram 49* probably refers to Marston.
[23] For the argument over this parody, see Appendix D.

This certainly sounds as though the writer had been reproved for the arrogance of his previous epilogue, and Marston's epilogue sounds as though it had furnished at least a part of that reproof.

It seems, then, that Jonson produced his Painter addition to the *Spanish Tragedy* about September, 1601, and that Marston soon after added to the stage version of *Antonio and Mellida* a parody upon it. About the same time he added an armed Epilogue which rebuked the Epilogue to *Cynthia's Revels* (written about the winter of 1600-1). This Epilogue of Marston's was in turn retorted to by the armed Prologue of the *Poetaster*.

It also seems probable that the Prologue of Shakespeare's *Troilus and Cressida*[24] referred to one or both these plays, but especially Jonson's:

> " . . . Hither am I come
> A prologue armed, — but not in confidence
> Of author's pen or actor's voice; but suited
> In like conditions as our argument." [25]

This mild reference is the only probable connection of Shakespeare's with the stage quarrel.[26]

[24] *Troilus and Cressida* was entered in the S. R. in 1603. The prologue, however, does not appear in the first quarto of 1609, but not until the First Folio.

Sidney Lee (*Shakespeare*, ed. 1899, p. 228, n.) believed that Shakespeare here distinctly disclaims all concern in the stage quarrel. This, on his own showing of dates (that is, that the play was written sometime before Feb. 7, 1602-3, when Roberts obtained his license) is more probable than his statement in the last edition (p. 371, n.): "*Troilus* cannot, on any showing, be assigned to the period of the war between Jonson, Dekker and Marston in 1601-2."

[25] That is, the armored Prologue was suited to the warlike nature of *Troilus and Cressida*. This was also the case with Andrugio in *Antonio and Mellida;* but Jonson's armed Prologue had no connection with the play.

[26] There is no sufficient reason for believing with Wyndham (*Poems of Shakespeare*, p. lxvii f.; Fleay, *Chron. Eng. Dra.* I, p. 366) that Thersites is drawn from Marston. For source of this character see Small, *Stage Quarrel*, p. 164-5; for good summing up of evidence, though no conclusion is reached, see Penniman's *War of Theatres*, pp. 144-150.

It is only for the sake of completeness that I here mention other supposed connections of Shakespeare with the quarrel. Wyndham

Professor Wallace[27] assigns Marston's *Dutch Courtezan* to the fall or winter of 1602, though he gives no reasons for changing the usually assigned date of 1604. At any rate, the *Dutch Courtezan* contains absolutely no notice of the quarrel, nor indeed any literary satire, unless the following be considered in the light of a retraction by the reconciled Marston: "Were I to bite an honest gentleman, a poor grograrian poet, or a penurious parson. . . I were doomed beyond the works of supererogation".[28] Probably no such reference was intended.

The Stage Quarrel was very definitely stopped at the time of the writing of Marston's Dedication to the *Malcontent*, 1604,[29] and his verses of commendation to Jonson's *Sejanus*, 1605. The fine Dedication reads: "Beniamino Ionsonio, Poetae elegantissimo, gravissimo, amico suo, candido et cordato, Ioannis Marston, musarum alumnus, asperam hanc suam Thaliam D [at] D [edicatque]."

(*Ibid. ff.*) first started the cry that Shakespeare's Pistol was intended to satirize Marston, and he was followed in full voice by the German critics (Sarrazin, *Beitr. rom. engl. philol.*, 1902, 182f.; C. Winkler, *Eng. Stud.* 1904, vol. 33, p. 218). The principal proofs are, that Jonson took Marston's pistol from him, hence Pistol must have been Marston's nickname; and, that Pistol used certain popular playscraps also quoted in Marston's plays. Comment seems unnecessary, notwithstanding the considerable amount of work spent in bolstering up the hypothesis.

Fleay (*Life and Work of Shakespeare*) says concerning *All's Well that Ends Well*, "I take the boasting Parolles to be Marston." Small (p. 138) has shown how little validity there is to the grounds he gives for his belief. Fleay says of *Twelfth Night* (p. 220), "I believe that Sir Toby represents Jonson and Malvolio Marston; but that subject requires to be treated in a separate work from its complexity." In *Shakespeariana* (I, 136) he undertakes to identify Malvolio with Malevole of the *Malcontent* and, says that "the mysterious M. O. A. I. of Maria's letter is an anagram of IO (HN) MA (RSTON)." This is the kind of conjecture valuable in proving that Bacon wrote Shakespeare.

[27] *Children of the Chapel.*

[28] III, ii, 38.

[29] Stoll has endeavored to advance the date of the *Malcontent* to 1600, though it certainly contains some allusions to James I and his new Scotch knights. However, the dedication would be written for the publication, not presentation of the play, which was entered July 5, 1604. Cf. infra, p. 143, n.

The Epilogue has another complimentary reference to Jonson[30].

After this reconciliation, however, the quarrel immediately broke out again. In 1606 Marston in the prefaces of two plays attacked Jonson on the old charges. Marston signed an address "To My[31] Equal Reader," prefixed to the *Fawn*:

"As for the factious malice and studied detractions of some few that tread in the same path with me, let all know I most easily neglect them . . . Of men of my own addiction I love most, pity some, hate none; for let me truly say it, I once only loved myself for loving them, and surely I shall ever rest so constant to my fine affection, and let their ungentle combinings, discourteous whisperings, never so treacherously labour to undermine my unfeared reputation, I shall (as long as I have being) love the least of their graces, and only pity the greatest of their vices."

This is made more definitely an attack on Jonson by a reference to *Sejanus* (pub. 1605) in the Address to the General Reader prefixed to Marston's *Sophonisba* (1606). The author has "not laboured in this poem to relate anything as an historian. . . To transcribe authors, quote authorities, and translate Latin prose orations into English blank verse, hath, in this subject, been the least aim of my studies," just as it had been one of the chief aims of Jonson's play.

Nothing is known of this fresh quarrel save these references, to which Jonson made no public reply.

In 1609 Dekker in his *Gull's Hornbook,* the chapter on How a Gallant should behave himself in a Playhouse, turns over the ashes of the quarrel. Better, he writes, than to twit

[30]"Then till another's happier Muse appears,
    To whose desertful lamps pleased Fates impart,
    Art above nature, judgment above art,
    Receive this piece . . . "

The 'happier Muse' must refer to the comedy of *Volpone,* which was to appear in 1605 or 6. (See Fleay and Holt, *Mod. Lang. Notes,* 1905). Jonson would have begun it soon after finishing *Sejanus,* 1603; his only intermediate dramatic work was his unimportant collaboration in *Eastward Ho.* Since the Epilogue requests silence, it is therefore evident that the *Malcontent* was being produced somewhere between 1603 and 1606. Though the Epilogue might possibly have been added at a revival of the play, still this forms an additional reason for doubting Stoll's early dating of the play.

[31] Bullen misprints it "*the*".

a poet with his red beard, little legs, and ash-colored feather (as Jonson had Crispinus-Marston in the *Poetaster*), or better than to toss him in a blanket (as Dekker had Horace-Jonson, at the end of *Satiromastix*), is to get up in the middle of his play and walk out. It is evident that Dekker here is indulging in reminiscences, and not making a fresh attack.

The anonymous Cambridge play, *The Return from Parnassus,* the second part, written about December-January, 1601-2, is interesting as containing our only important outside reference to the stage quarrel. It includes a direct criticism of Marston, and a character, called Furor Poeticus, which has been said[32] to represent him. The direct reference occurs near the beginning of the play,[33] in a long passage where contemporary poets are being passed in review.

INGENIOSO. John Marston.
JUDICIO. What, Monsieur Kinsayder, lifting up your leg and pissing
    against the world? put up, man, put up for shame.
Methinks he's a ruffian in his style,
Withouten bands or garters' ornament.
He quaffs a cup of Frenchman's Helicon.
The roister-doister in his oily terms
Cuts, thrusts, and foins at whomsoever he meets,
And strows about Ram Alley meditations.
Tut, what cares he for modest, close-coucht terms,
Cleanly to gird our looser libertines?
Give him plain, naked words stript from their shirts,
That might beseem plain-dealing Aretine.
Ay, there is one that backs a paper steed
And manageth a penknife gallantly;
Strikes his poinado at a button's breadth;
Brings the great battering-ram of terms to towns,
And at first volley of his cannon-shot,
Batters the walls of the old fusty world."

This shows that Marston appeared to men of his own day precisely as he does to us, an exaggerated satirist, sometimes without decency but with a good deal of power; and a 'ruffian in his style'.

It is not easy to assign a definite place to Furor Poeticus, who seems the nearest of the characters to Marston. He had

---

[32] Fleay, *Chr.* II, 352.
[33] In orig. qto., sheet B2.

formerly been a student at Cambridge[34] with Phantasma; they
are always represented as being together, and Phantasma
frequently directs the thoughts of Furor.[35] When Ingenioso-
Nash's[36] exile to the Isle of Dogs is being discussed[37], Philo-
musus asks:

> "But say, what shall become of Furor and Phantasma?
> INGEN. These my companions still with me must wend.
> ACAD. Fury and Fancy on good wits attend."

It is evident that sometimes they are thought of as being
allegorical; at other times, they are certain students, filled with
poetry and fancy.[38] Occasionally, from the style and references of Furor, it would seem that the author had Marston
in mind. In III, iv some particularly Marstonian words are
used:

"Howe'er my dulled intellectual
Capres less nimbly than it did before . . .
INGEN. Nay, prithee, good Furor, do not rove in rhymes before thy
time: thou hast a very terrible roaring muse, nothing but squib
and fine jerks, quiet thyself awhile . . .
FUROR. I'll shake his heart upon my verses' point,
Rip out his guts with riving poinard,
Quarter his credit with a bloody quill.
PHAN. Calami, atramentum, charta, libelli,
Sunt semper studiis arma parata tuis.
INGEN. Enough, Furor, we know thou art a nimble swaggerer with
a goose quill."

Compare this with the criticism of Marston quoted from the
beginning of the play, and with Jonson's parody of Marston.
"whereas, our intellectual, or mincing capreal",[39] both Marstonian words.

Later[40] Furor is represented as using high-flown terms, until
the old knight exclaims, "Precious coals, . . . it's even so,
he is either a mad man or a conjuror; it is well if his words
were examined, to see if they be the Queen's or no."

[34] V, iv.
[35] As in I, vi.
[36] See Schelling, *Eliz. Drama*, II, 67 for identification.
[37] V, iv.
[38] In certain passages Furor recalls Lily (I, vi; V, iv).
[39] Clove, in *Every Man Out*, III, i.
[40] IV, ii.

Furor is not Marston; he is poor, conceited, from Cambridge, much more full of poetic or near-poetic afflatus than he can hold. But there are so many correspondences between his poetry and that of Marston, in the use of words and unpleasant phrases; and the play's criticism of Marston is so similar in tone to its criticism of Furor, that I feel sure Marston was at times in the writer's mind, and that we have here an exaggerated Marstonese spirit of poetry held up to ridicule. Thus light is thrown upon the contemporary attitude toward Marston's work and style. Jonson was not alone in his censure — the ordinary reader of the time must have felt the absurdity of some of Marston's work, but at the same time must have been impressed by his vigor and stinging satire.

SUMMARY

We find, then, that Marston's part in the stage quarrel extended from some time, probably late, in 1599, to late in 1601, peace being signed in Marston's dignified Latin dedication to Jonson of the *Malcontent* in 1604. A later quarrel found but slight expression on the stage.

In *Histriomastix*, 1599, Marston had satirized Monday in the figure of Posthaste, and had introduced some satiric allusions to Jonson, in the depiction of the hero of the play, Chrisoganus. Jonson, who apparently had taken umbrage, slipped some abuse of Marston's vocabulary into *Every Man Out of his Humour*, just at the beginning of the century; he even went to the extent of mentioning the word *Histriomastix*. Later in the same year Marston retorted by defending the gulls whom Jonson had displayed for ridicule in the Humour plays; he showed the guller himself gulled, in the character of Brabant Senior, who, incidentally, appreciates no one's poetry but his own. This was in *Jack Drum's Entertainment*, which included nothing that we would call a real impersonation of any literary figure, in spite of the multitude of conjectures which have been expended. This is also true of Jonson's *Cynthia's Revels*, written about the same time, save that in it Jonson displayed himself as Crites, and held enemies of Crites up to ridicule.

Marston came nearer towards bringing his antagonist *in propria persona* on the stage, by his character of Lampatho in *What You Will,* in 1601. Just as *Jack Drum* had been a reply to *Every Man Out* and its guller, so ostensibly *What You Will* was a similar reply to *Cynthia's Revels* and its detraction of the court. But Brabant Senior in the former had not been really a portrait of Jonson, save in one or two particulars, mostly matters of art-opinion; while Lampatho in *What You Will* was practically Jonson brought upon the stage.

Jonson replied within fifteen weeks with the invective of *Poetaster,* where he abused Marston to the utmost of his power, and showed him on the stage in a degrading caricature. Dekker was pilloried by his side, perhaps because Jonson had gotten wind of the fact that Dekker was writing a play against him. What brought Dekker into the quarrel at this point is uncertain; it may have been that he was simply hired by Marston and some others, especially actors, whom theatrical reasons and Jonson's arrogance had angered. He was always a playwright-to-let, and he probably was not unwilling to take a try at lowering Jonson's overweening pride.

Directly after the *Poetaster* appeared Dekker's *Satiromastix;* in its conception Marston probably had a hand, though he does not seem to have written any of it. Here the tables were turned on Horace-Jonson, and he got as good as he had given, with apparently a greater popular result.

It is possible that Jonson was warned by the authorities to desist, or perhaps popular opinion was too strongly against him; at any rate he made no reply save for his *Apologetical Dialogue,* appended to his play when it was printed in 1602. Toward the end of 1601 Marston burlesqued a scene of Jonson's additions to the *Spanish Tragedy,* in a passage inserted in *Antonio and Mellida.* The conflict was formally ended in 1604 with the Dedication of Marston's *Malcontent* to Jonson, though in 1606 there are traces of a revival in Marston's Prologues to the *Fawn* and *Sophonisba.*

The quarrel thus took place in the main in seven plays, three of Marston's, three of Jonson's, and finally one of Dekker's inspired by Marston. From the mere hints of its beginnings it increased in vehemence to what was really its climax, the word-vomiting of the *Poetaster.* The 'poetasters' nevertheless had the best of it in the popular opinion of the time, and today also it seems that they were more offended than offending, to judge from the only evidence we possess, the plays.

There would have been no personal quarrel had it not been for Jonson's arrogance, and this arrogance was the cause of his failure. They were alleging the truth while he was showering abuse.

Thus the enormous 'War of the Theatres' which has been gradually evolved by the critics, is reduced to comparatively modest proportions. There were certain other personal allusions to poets in other plays of the time, but they are, I believe, much fewer in number and harder to prove than has been assumed, and we know of answers on the stage by no one save Marston and Dekker. Whatever division into two camps of playwrights there may have been, sprung from the rivalry of the children's companies, and was but ephemeral. In the seven plays that have been discussed, however, we have a definite series of provocation and attack, rebuttal and rejoinder, steadily increasing in animosity until the fight was undisguised in the *Poetaster* and *Satiromastix*.

Marston's work in the satire was inspired by the literary fashion of the times in which they were produced. In order to understand his 'scourging of villainy', it is necessary to bear in mind the trend of satiric history.

Of the Elizabethan critics, perhaps Puttenham[2] comes nearest to giving a definition of satire, when he writes, "The first and most bitter invective against vice and vicious men, was the Satyre;" the word satire he explains as coming from the fact that, for the sake of anonymity, the first reciters of satires appeared disguised at Satyrs. Perhaps the best definition of formal satire would be one adapted from Heinsius[3]: 'Formal satire is a kind of non-narrative poetry in which human faults are reprehended, and erring classes or individuals, the latter usually under assumed names, are made hateful

[1] Mr. R. M. Alden has admirably gone over the ground of English formal satires, in his *Rise of Formal Satire in England under Classical Influence*, (*Pub. of U. of Penn. in Philol. etc.*, Vol. VI, No. 2. Philadelphia, 1899). It is unfortunate that he should have been obliged strictly to limit the scope of his work to formal satire, thereby shutting out much satiric material. I know of nothing of importance written upon the epigrammatic form of satire, which at times so closely approaches the longer kind that if epigrams on like subjects had been joined, the result would have been no other than formal satire. Thus Martial drew upon Juvenal and Persius for part of his material; and Elizabethan epigrammatists such as John Davies and Weever were doing exactly the same thing as Donne and Hall, save in the outward form in which their works were presented. Likewise we have in longer, looser form the half-narrative poems such as the *Pasquil* productions of about 1612; T. N's. *Barleybreak, or warning for wantons*, 1607; and Parke's *Curtaine Drawer of the World*, 1612; these are in their whole intention satiric. (These may be found in Grosart's *Occasional Issues.*) Again, there are the very numerous prose productions of the time, including the many by Lodge, Nash, Greene and Dekker, which differ from formal satire mostly in running to greater length, and describing as well as denouncing. Finally, the vast field of dramatic satire has never been treated at any length.

[2] *Art of Poesie*, I, xiii.

[3] *Dissertations on Horace.* Quoted by Dryden, in his famous *Essay on Satire*, whence Alden quotes it, (p. 2.)

or ridiculous.' Each satire usually attacks a single vice under several different aspects.

There was a considerable amount of informal satire in earlier English literature, such as Chaucer's, Langland's and Skelton's, but formal satire did not appear until it was produced by direct emulation of the classic satire. The dependence of the Elizabethan satirists, more especially the formal satirists and epigrammatists, upon the Latin classics was well nigh absolute. The most cursory reading of Donne, Hall, Lodge, in conjunction with Horace, Juvenal, Martial, reveals an astonishing lack of originality of the Elizabethans in this regard. Often they did not even attempt to adopt Roman satire to English ways, but with the classic names which they affected, took over classic manners[4]. Thus we find little development of the form, when once the classic model was adopted: Donne's satires of 1593, at the beginning of the vogue of satires, are little different in form or subject matter from those of Fitzgeffrey, writing after Shakespeare's death. The only important change was introduced by Wither, about 1613, who enlarged on the moral and impersonal side, and who had great influence on succeeding satirists.

Formal satire in England really began with Sir Thomas Wyatt, who wrote three poems of this sort about 1541-2. They were stoic in character, and were based especially on Horace, though the second poem is from the Italian Alamanni. These poems, although in reality satires, were not so called until modern times. Wyatt's friend the Earl of Surrey in 1543 wrote a poem called a *Satire Against the Citizens of London,* which is hardly a satire at all, but rather a moralizing poem.

Omitting unimportant works,—the first English satires to be given that name were those by Edward Hake in 1567: *News*

---

[4] See the third satire of Hall's third book, Martial writ large, where he sets forth a Roman menu, and the next satire, on ostentation, which begins:

"Were yesterday Polemon's natals kept,
That so his threshold is all freshly steept
With new-shed blood? Could he not sacrifice
Some sorry morkin that unbidden dies? etc."

The sixth satire, also from Martial, concerns a drunkard drinking up Acheron.

85

out of Powles Churchyarde . . . Written in English Satyrs. Wherein is reprooved excessive and unlawfull seeking after riches, and the evill spending of the same. Hake's sources were English, not classical. The most influential of the early satires was *The Steele Glas. A Satyre compiled by George Gascoigne, Esquire, in 1576.* It was written in an unusual vehicle for satire, blank verse. This too is essentially a moral poem rather than a true satire,—that is, its method is to stimulate virtue directly, rather than by exposing vice. The steel glass was represented as the kind used in the good old days, which did not flatter. The poem condemns riches and luxury, and judges the several stations and professions of life; the epilogue attacks the luxurious women of the time. The only distinct source seems to be *Piers Ploughman,* which it mentions with praise.

Nearly a score of years passed between the *Steele Glas* and the beginning of the flood of satires which swept over England near the close of the sixteenth century. John Donne seems to have been the originator, beginning to write his satires about 1593, when he was a youth of twenty. There is a MS of that date containing three satires, and all seven were completed shortly after the accession of James I. Though none of them are known to have appeared in print until the first edition of Donne's poems, 1633, they were certainly widely known shortly after they were written, and they set the tone for their successors.[5] The first satire attacks a 'humourous' courtier—that is, a creature of whims; incidentally it attacks snobbery, lust and self-conceit. The next two deal with lawyers and religious sectaries. The fourth is the Horatian satire, later used in the *Poetaster,* of the assiduity of a bore; affectations of language and dress, and the court, are also satirized. The other satires utilize Juvenal and to a less degree Persius as sources. Donne's use of the heroic couplet for his satires probably determined the verse form employed by most of his successors; Lodge seems to have used it independently at about the same time.

[5] From internal evidence, the first four were written before Hall's book of 1597, with his claim to be the first English satirist. The fact that Hall's satires are more often mentioned arises simply from their having been published, while Donne's were not. But Donne's had at least as great an influence.

Thomas Lodge, the playwright, poet, pamphleteer and doctor, included four satires in his *Fig for Momus,* published in 1595.[6] In his address *To the Gentlemen Readers whatsoever,* he claims priority in writing satires, epistles and eclogues:

"I have thought good to include *Satyres, Eclogues and Epistles* . . . because I would write in that forme, wherein no man might chalenge me with servile imitation . . . My *Satyres* (to speake truth) are, by pleasures, rather placed here to prepare and trie the eare then to feed it; because, if it passe well, the whole centon of them. alreadie in my hands, shall sodainly be published."

Apparently the *Fig for Momus* did not "passe well", for no more of his satires appeared, though their mention by Meres in 1598 indicates some fame.[7] He goes on,

"In them (under the name of certaine Romaines) where I reprehend vice, I purposely wrong no man, but observe the lawes of that kind of poeme. If any repine thereat, I am sure he is guiltie. because he bewrayeth himself."

He is here, thus early, speaking of the formal satire as having a fixed shape and being governed by certain laws, evidently those to be deduced from the classics. We find Juvenal to have been his principal source; as in previous satires, there is a minimum of reference to contemporary life.

In 1597 the first three books of Hall's satires were printed. In 1598 appeared his last three books, Marston's *Pygmalion and certain Satyres* and his *Scourge of Villainy,* and Edward Guilpin's *Skialetheia: or, a Shadowe of Truth in certain Epigrams and Satyres.* This last was entered on the Stationers' Register September 15, a few days later than Marston's *Scourge of Villainy,* and was evidently written with a knowledge of Marston's work. He also knew Hall and Donne, and had unusually little dependence upon classical sources.

In the next year, 1599, besides perhaps three further editions of Hall's[8] and two of Marston's satires, appeared *Micro-*

[6] The book also included seven Epistles and four Eclogues.
[7] "With us, in the same faculty of satire, these are chief: *Piers Ploughman, Lodge, Hall* of Emmanuel College in Cambridge; *the author of Pygmalion's Image and certain Satires; the author of Skialtheia."* *Palladis Tamia,* reprinted in Arber's *English Garner,* p. 100.
[8] For bibliography of Hall's *Virgidemiarum* see *Die Satiren Halls,* Konrad Schulze, *Palaestra* cvi, pp. 4 and 7.

cynicon, Sixe Snarling Satyres, which has been doubtfully assigned to Thomas Middleton. If so, it is his first literary work, as satires had been Marston's first. *Micro-cynicon* shows knowledge of both Hall and Marston. This same year came the order of the Archbishop of Canterbury and the Bishop of London, for the burning of the satires of Hall, Marston, Guilpin, and the *Micro-cynicon.*[9] That this occurence had an effect upon Marston's reputation is shown by the entry in the Stationers' Register for *Antonio and Mellida,* October 24, 1601; the play was to be entered "Provided that he can get lawfull license for yt", which shows him still under suspicion. Perhaps it was of his own case Marston was thinking when he wrote in the *Dutch Courtezan*[10]

"For as in the fashion of time those books that are called in are most in sale and request, so in nature those actions that are most prohibited are most desired."[11]

PYGMALION

It was this tide of fashion which directed Marston's earliest work toward satire. But the long poem at the beginning of his first thin volume[12] was not apparently satiric at all, though the author so called it. It was in another favorite vein of the day, a narrative poem giving a poetic rendering of a classic love story. We have many of the same genre, most of them drawing their material from Ovid's *Metamorphoses.*[13]

[9] Fleay (*Life of Shakespeare,* p. 208) attempts to date *As You Like It* soon after this occurrence, by the line "The little wit fools have was silenced" (I, ii, 94), which he believes alludes to this burning.

[10] III, i, 44.

[11] This passage is a borrowing from Florio's Montaigne, III, v: "It is not herein as in matters of books, which being once called in and forbidden become more saleable and public."

[12] *The Metamorphosis of Pymalions Image, and Satyres,* entered in S. R. May 27, 1598, and published the same year. This edition Grosart places among "the many that appear to have been in continuous circulation" — merely guesswork, as there is no evidence of any other edition. *Pygmalion's Image,* without the *Satyres,* was reprinted with *Alcilia, Philoparthen's loving Folly, Love of Amos and Laura,* etc., in 1613 and 1628 (Bullen, *Marston,* I, xvii).

[13] Perhaps the first was Thomas Peend's *Salmacis and Hermaphroditus,* 1565. Among others later were Grove's *Pelops and Hippodamia,*

Critics have been sharply divided as to the satiric element in *Pygmalion's Image*. These are the facts. No one reading the poem would for a moment suspect that it was meant as satire or contained any hidden meaning at all.[14] There is nothing in the dedication, "To the World's Mighty Monarch, Good Opinion", in the Argument of the Poem, or even in the address "To his Mistress" (though that seems to be in a somewhat less serious vein) that would lead one to suspect that *Pygmalion* was not what it purported to be, a frankly amorous poem, like a dozen of the same kind that had preceded it. It is not until we come to "The Author in praise of his precedent Poem", placed between the poem and the satires, that we first discover that the author is not taking his work seriously. This is more directly personal, and from its tone is evidently more akin to the satires than to the poem. It is written in heroic couplets, like the satires, while the poem is in six-line stanzas. It employs typical language of the satires:

> "Now, Rufus, by old Glebron's fearful mace,
> Hath not my muse deserved a worthy place?
> Come, come, Luxurio, crown my head with bays,
> Which, like a Paphian, wantonly displays
> The Salaminion titillations
> Which tickle up our lewd Priapians."

He goes on to deride his address to his mistress, and tries to connect the poem's happy ending with some other contemporary work:

etc., 1587; Thomas Lodge's *Glaucus and Scylla, or Scylla's Metamorphosis*, 1589; Shakespeare's *Venus and Adonis*, Marlowe's and Chapman's *Hero and Leander*, Samuel Daniel's *Complaint of Rosamund* (with an English story), 1593; about this time were written Gervaise Markham's lost *Thyrsis and Daphne*, and Henry Constable's *Sheepheard's Song of Venus and Adonis* (first published 1600, but perhaps written before Shakespeare's poem); Richard Barnfield's *Affectionate Shepherd*, Shakespeare's *Rape of Lucrece*, 1594; Chapman's *Ovid's Banquet of Sense*, Drayton's *Endymion and Phoebe*, Edwards' *Cephalus and Procris*, and his *Narcissus*, 1595. But by 1598 the fashion seems to have been dying out. For later examples, see infra, p. 121, n.

[14] Certainly it required unusual perspicuity to discern that "the wooing of Adonis by the queen of love (i. e., Shakespeare's poem) is very roughly but very cleverly parodied." Anon. in *Enc. Brit.* 9th ed., XV, 575. Not repeated in 11th ed.

> "So Labeo did complain his love was stone . . .
> Yet Lynceus knows that in the end of this
> He[15] wrought as strange a metamorphosis.
> Ends not my poem then surpassing ill?"[16]

He concludes by saying that he censures himself, so disarming criticism:

> "My lines are froth, my stanzas sapless be . . .
> Ye changing Proteans, list,
> And tremble at a barking satirist."

Then follows the first satire. Thus "The Author in praise" is evidently a device for transition from the poem to the satires; it furnishes primarily an introduction to them rather than a serious criticism of *Pygmalion*.

In the sixth satire of the *Scourge of Villainy* Marston elaborates this view of his poem. *Pygmalion* has been censured:

> "Curio, knowst my sprite,
> Yet deem'st that in sad seriousness I write
> Such nasty stuff as is *Pygmalion?*
>   Ha, how he glavers with his fawning snout,
> And swears he thought I meant but faintly flout
> My fine smug rhyme . . .
> Hence, thou misjudging censor: know I wrote
> Those idle rhymes to note the odious spot
> And blemish that deforms the lineaments
> Of modern poesie's habiliments."

Thas is, *Pygmalion* was written as a burlesque on the poetry of the day.

Altogether, Marston devotes some eighty lines of this satire to *Pygmalion,* roundly asserting that it was satire; and still, few feel completely satisfied that the poem was conceived satirically. As Grosart says, Marston here gives "a kind of apology for *Pygmalion,* albeit more ingeniously than ingenuously." And Winkler[17] writes truly, "das alle Versuche

---

[15] I. e., Labeo, whom I take to indicate here some complaining sonnetteer, impossible to identify, and certainly not Hall, who wrote no love-poetry. Lynceus is always used by Marston to indicate the sharp-sighted observer.

[16] L. 29f.

[17] *John Marston's litterarische Anfange.* Dissertation. Carl Wilhelm Winckler. Breslau, 1903. P. 38.

Marstons, den *Pygmalion* als satirische Dichtung hinzustellen, an den Tatsachen selbst scheitern. Während er zuerst (in *the Author in praise* u.s.w.) seine eigene Dichtung ganz zutreffend als lasciv brandmarkt, aber den beweis schuldig bleibt und bleiben muss, dass die zeitgenössische Litteratur denselben Charakter trage, kennzeichnet er später (in *Scourge* o. V. VI,) eine Reihe von Swächen seiner Zeitgenossen ganz richtig, ohne sie indessen, wie er behauptet, in *Pygmalion* verspottet zu haben."

Elsewhere, Marston himself states that he had written amorous poetry. Satire II opens,

> "I that even now lisp'd like an amorist
> Am turned into a snaphance[18] satirist,"

and he goes on to say that he has not been immaculate. In all probability he is referring to *Pygmalion*.

It is not difficult to conjecture what probably happened. *Pygmalion* was Marston's first work, just as *Venus and Adonis* was the first heir of Shakespeare's invention. Perhaps it was written when Marston was in college, at the time when the vogue of the amorous poem was at its height; at the very latest, Marston could not have been more than about twenty-two at its composition. It was indeed, conventionally erotic. Though Marston went further than most of his contemporaries in the use of daring language, we feel that he himself while writing was never emotionally carried away; the poem is always cold and intellectual.[19]

Later, after he had lived in London, he easily fell into the prevailing satiric fashion. Perhaps after his first satires had been composed, the publication of Hall's *Virgidemiarum* prompted him to bring out what he had written, and the earlier poem was utilized to fill out the book;[20] probably Marston, though by this time somewhat ashamed of it, really desired its

---

[18] Hair-trigger.

[19] We are reminded of the temper of Swift's erotic poetry, which, however, is obviously satirical.

[20] As in Hake's satires, *News out of Powles Churchyarde*, with its notice: "Gentle Reader, for the fillings up of emptie pages, this letter written by the Author to his friends lying at the point of death is inserted." Other instances are of course frequent in Elizabethan literature, as in some of Lodge's and Greene's tracts.

publication, as his first work. Since its character was obviously just that which the accompanying satires attacked, he connected the two by satiric lines which made fun of the poem. This evidently did not disarm contemporary critics, who rightly thought he 'meant but faintly flout his fine smug verse'. So he braved out the attempt at denial in the *Scourge of Villainy*, explaining faults of matter and manner by saying that they were intentional, and even hinting, though not actually asserting, that the *Pygmalion* contained definite hits at contemporary poetry. These have been sought for, of course vainly, by modern critics.[21] In brief, Marston first ridiculed his own poem to reconcile it with the satires, and was later drawn on to try to make it seem a parody, which the poem evidently was not.

FORMAL SATIRES

Marston wrote sixteen formal satires, besides preliminary and concluding matter. Five of these were in the volume entitled *The Metamorphosis of Pygmalion's Image; and Certain Satires;* ten were in the first edition of the *Scourge of Villainy*, and one more was added to its second edition. The *Scourge of Villainy* is divided into three books, for no apparent reason save imitation of the classics; these books contain four, three and four satires respectively. If any generalization can be attempted where none seems to have been designed, it may be said that the *Satires* treat generally of hypocrisy; the first book of the Scourge, of lust; the second, of man's general depravity; and the third, of his minor faults. Altogether the satires, etc., take 2757 lines,[22] thus allowing room for a great variety of attack. It will be my aim to classify the objects of Marston's satire, and to show briefly his apparent attitude toward his surroundings, at least as far as he chose to put it in his satires.

The subjects of Marston's satire may be divided[23] into six large and not too clearly defined groups: First, general,

[21] Winckler, Ibid.; Grosart.
[22] Bullens ed. This number does not include the poem of *Pygmalion*. Cf. Gascoigne's *Steele Glas*, about 1140 lines; Hake's *Newes Out of Powles*, about 2800 short lines; Donne's *Satires*, 713; Lodge's, 395; Hall's, 2812.
[23] Generally following Alden.

including the nature and mission of satire itself, the wretched state of the world, and the degeneracy of the age; second, morals, including hypocrisy, lust, religion, and the varieties of crime; third, humours, or what we might today call exaggerated hobbies and idiosyncracies; fourth, manners and fashion, as of clothes, eating and drinking; fifth, classes of mankind — including woman; and finally, sixth, literature.

GENERAL SATIRE

Perhaps the most baffling problem connected with Marston is that of discovering what his own attitude toward life really was. Generally Marston seems in deadly earnest in scourging an useless world; at times he laughs at the follies of the world; again he confesses that it was all make-believe:

> "Though angry brow was bent,
> Yet have I sung in sporting merriment."

He pitches the general key of his satire very high. The satirist he takes to be a missionary, a kind of Scourge of God for the chastisement of the times. I do not think Marston really believed this; but he thought it was the proper tone for Satire to adopt, because he was following Hall's magniloquent example, the only English satirist he knew. Hall had written, for example, in this vein:[24]

> "Nay, no despite: but angry Nemesis
> Whose scourge doth follow all that done amiss:
> That scourge I bear, albe in ruder fist,
> And wound, and strike, and pardon whom she list."

Hence it is that Marston derives the inspiration of such lines as:[25]

> "Now, grim Reproof, swell in my rough-hued rhyme,
> That thou mayst vex the guilty of our time."

> "Now doth Rhamnusia Adrastian,
> Daughter of Night, and of the Ocean,
> Provoke my pen. What cold Saturnian
> Can hold, and hear such vile detraction?"

[24] *Virgid.* Prol. to Lib. II.
[25] S. iii. 1. Other passages of the same tenor are *Author in Praise; SV. In Lect.* 38; *Proem,* Lib. I; I, 43; II, 1; 37; 70; 80; III, 126; V, 103; VI, 13; Pr. in Lib. III; IX, 1; 126.

This last[26] is a parody of Hall's Defiance to Envy, but other passages[27] show how Marston went from parody to imitation:

"I bear the scourge of just Rhamnusia,
Lashing the lewdness of Britannia."

"Grim-faced Reproof, sparkle with threatening eye!
Bend thy sour brows in my tart poesy!
Avaunt, ye curs! howl in some cloudy mist,
Quake to behold a sharp-fanged satirist!"

Marston derived this sort of thing from Hall, and Hall from Seneca, not from the classic satirists. Juvenal it is true had something of the spirit, but it was expressed in a very different form. The Senecan rhodomontade was introduced into English satire by Hall,[28] for it is not found in Gascoigne, Hake, Lodge or Donne. Marston adopted and over-used it, until every reader is inclined to rebel at the high-mightiness of his self-constituted authority.

His general attitude is that the world has become altogether degenerate, and is now in a frightful state. He speaks not in admonition, but in shrill abhorrence, which he continually says he cannot restrain himself from expressing.[29] Even when he laughs at mankind's follies, it is such violent, bitter laughter that again and again he has to beware of 'breaking his gall'.[30] Marston's theory of the cause of the time's evilness was that the connection between God and man had been interrupted; the union between soul and body had therefore been broken, and the body was left to its bestiality. He expresses this in characteristic terms: Goodness was piped into man from the Deity, but the slime from our natural souls "Have stopped those pipes by which it was conveyed", and

[26] S. iv. 1.
[27] *Proem*, Lib. I; *SV*. IX, 1.
[28] Cf. Prologue to Lib. I, *Virgid*.
[29] So he heads one of the satires with a quotation from Juvenal, "Difficile est Satiram non scribere." SV. II contains a number of such statements.
[30] S. i, 51, where Democritus laughs at a foolish lover — a forerunner of Burton's Democritus Junior; cf. also SV.II, 80. For violent laughter, cf. S. i, 51, 124; iii, 71, 81; SV. XI, 12, 239. For classical sources of this hilarity at folly or vice, cf. Juvenal X, 33; Persius, I, 12.

now 'the blessed Synderesis' which united the soul and body of man has vanished.[31]

Naturally he has the greatest contempt for most of his readers, for whom his book is much too good:

> "What though the sacred issue of my soul
> I here expose to idiots' control "[32]

> "Nay then, come all; I prostitute my muse,
> For all the swarms of idiots to abuse." [33]

Marston's satire is direct; he has no ability to use such finer tools as irony.[34] Once he attempts it in a clumsy way: vice is so prosperous that the satirist must have been deceived into taking wrong for right, hell for heaven; if that be the case he has nothing further to satirise. But he confesses his inability to deal further in the vein:

> "Now doth my satire stagger in a doubt,
> Whether to cease or else to write it out.
> The subject is too sharp for my dull quill."[35]

Nevertheless he uses a sort of irony when attempting to forestall the criticism which his work would provoke. Hall had written a *Defiance to Envy*, which Marston read very carefully, first in order to parody, then to imitate, though giving it his own peculiar twist. His first work, *Pygmalion*, had been dedicated "To the World's mighty Monarch, Good Opinion," and his first edition of the *Scourge*, "To his most esteemed and best beloved Self." In 1599 he dedicated the *Scourge of Villainy* to Detraction. We see here a change of tactics; his state of mind at first was that of the young author anxious for praise and afraid of censure; his dedication to himself shows him, stung by criticism, attempting to fall back upon himself and disdain whatever the world said; the dedica-

---

[31] SV. VII, XI.

[32] SV. VI, 105; cf. SV. IV, 167f.

[33] SV. In Lect: 61. Cf. the attitude in the Preface to Chapman's *Ovid's Banquet of Sense*, and toward the end of *Every Man Out* (quoted, Baskerville, p. 313).

[34] This is another reason for doubting that all *Pygmalion* was intended as a gigantic piece of irony.

[35] S. v. 139f.

tion to Detraction itself may well show him as driven out of wouldbe isolation into a blustering attempt to show that he desired censure. It is evident from the number of times he mentions his reputation as author[36] that he was greatly interested, and this Dedication to Detraction was only his characteristic device to avoid danger by flattering it. So it was that on his tombstone appeared "Oblivioni Sacrum". Marston was the Malcontent, taking shelter in the tyrant's very court and favour, till time should serve for revenge.

MORALS

Under this heading are included, first and most important, lust, with its several varieties; hypocrisy, and the love of money include most of the other objects of attack.

Lust is the most prominent subject of Marston's literary work. He began by writing *Pygmalion*, the most frank in its wording of any of the erotic Elizabethan poems. As for his plays, the briefest reading makes it only too evident how engaged the dramatist's mind was with the flesh. So, it is not surprising that attacks on lechery fill the main part of his satires. They begin with it, for *The Author in Praise*, following *Pygmalion*, is really the satire's preface. Its purpose is to try to make *Pygmalion* appear a satire too, and one on sensual poetry, to "tickle up our lewd Priapians". General attacks on lust are everywhere in the *Satires* themselves. In the *Scourge of Villainy*, satires I, III, and VII are principally concerned

---

[36] Detraction is warned from his work, SV. VI, 101, and a slanderer is satirized, SV. I, 64. He especially accuses Hall of detraction, S. iv, 4, 109. In the *Author in Praise*, following *Pygmalion*, he tries to disarm criticism by proclaiming his own faults: he will

"Censure myself, 'fore others me deride . . .
My lines are froth, my stanzas sapless be."

(This sounds as though it might mask the beginning of his change of mind about *Pygmalion*. At first he may have thought to reconcile it thus with the Satires, by admitting its faults. Certainly he is not here thinking that the poem was intended to be a parody.)

Bullen in a note says he fails to understand why Marston signed the last of his *Satires*, Epictetus. It probably is to be explained by a passage in the preface to the *Fawn:* "My bosom friend, good Epictetus, makes me easily to contemn all such men's malice." (Cf. also the mention of Epictetus in the *Proemium in Lib. II, SV.*)

with it, as are large parts of IV, VIII and XI; and it is constantly alluded to even when it is not the theme, indeed when the immediate object of attack seems quite foreign, as gambling, embezzling or stupidity.[37]

When lust is so carefully and lingeringly dwelt upon, it is impossible to avoid the suspicion that its consideration was pleasing to the author. There is no reason for doubting that such was the case. From his own day to this, his readers have been shocked, or at least displeased, because Marston is so vivid in his frankness, his eagerness to reveal strikingly facts usually left unmentioned, at least by art. He has the ability and the desire to retail graphically and forcibly all the ugly details of illicit sexual relations. One naturally wonders how this teacher recked his own rede, but we cannot answer; we know nothing of Marston's private life or morals save what we can glean from his own works. He certainly displays a large and varied knowledge of depravity. Heinsius called satire a kind of poetry 'invented for the purging of our minds', and it may have had this effect upon its writer.

Marston's satires do not effect their avowed and real purpose — that of punishing and so lessening vice — because his readers are not as coldblooded as the author. It is true that he nearly always puts vice in an unpleasant light — certainly sensual vice. So far he fulfills well enough the demand of literary morality, that nothing be written which tends "to debase the affections, sophisticate or deaden the conscience, enfeeble the will".[38] But readers are diverted from disliking the vice to disliking the scourge, — and so, in spite of his undeniable power of phrasing, Marston is little read. It is largely a matter of taste, and good taste he utterly offends. Contemporary criticism, as in the *The Whipping of the Satire* and *The Return from Parnassus*, shows even the less fastidious canons of Elizabethan taste were transgressed. And it is no wonder that in 1887 Mr. Bullen mentioned a fleeting doubt concerning a possible censoring of his reprint of Marston. Marston, like Swift, frequently connected lust and bodily filth; and this combination, when expressed as forcibly and effectively as his genius enabled him to write, is only too likely to be more than modern sensibility can stomach.

[37] SV. IV, 88; 8; VIII, 165.
[38] Winchester, *Principles of Lit. Crit.*, p. 111.

As might be expected, Marston does not hesitate to speak freely of almost every variety of sexual vice. Whores of all ranks are given considerable attention. He has none of Ford's and the modern world's sentimental pity for their fallen estate; in his eyes they are thoroughly evil, bringing the downfall of men, and they are what they are simply because "modesty is roosted in the skies".[39] But his principal interest is in men. He not only warns them in too forceful words from whores,[40] but condemns them bitterly for their open lewdness. One satire[41] dwells almost entirely on this subject, of men's souls lost through "riot, lust, and fleshly seeming-sweetness". Elizabethan morals were far from rigid, but if they were as openly vicious as the satirist attempts to show, England would have vied with Imperial Rome.[42] Indeed, Marston's tone is more that of Juvenal here than anywhere else; yet he seems to have taken almost no details from the classics. Cuckolds and adulterers are mentioned in the usual Elizabethan terms: the citizen more or less unwillingly allows his wife to be seduced by the courtier;[43] but in addition Marston seems to have had an attraction toward the mentioning of incest and various family confusions.[44] Homosexuality is unsparingly dealt with,[45] and he utters the customary complaint against travellers, that they bring in "beastly luxuries, Some hell-devised lustful villainies; Even apes and beasts would blush with

[39] SV. II, 109. Some references to this subject are: S. ii, 107; SV. In Lect. 12; I, 15; 56 (cf. *Virgid.* IV, 1: "all day simpering"); III, 29; VIII, 172; IX, 121; XI, 199.
[40] SV. II, 38f.
[41] SV. VII.
[42] S. i, 90, 98, 107; ii, 118; SV. *In Lect.* 76, refer to the dissolute soldier Tubrio. For other references, see esp. SV. I, 60, 71, 38f; III, 88, 91, 139, 189; IV, 8, 33, 88; V, 82, 90; VII passim; VIII, 118f; XI, 137.
[43] S. i, 55, 63; SV. I, 73f; III, 99, 185; V, 78; XI, 115, 167.
[44] SV. I, 37, 60; III, 95, 184; V, 97. In X, 27 a younger cuckolds an elder brother, and by the consequent birth of an heir loses his inheritance; this incident is expanded in the *Fawn*, IV, i, 73, 90.
[45] S. iii, 33; SV. II, 49; III, 38f., 58-68, where he says that from its source at Douai seminary it has spread to 'Valladolid our Athens', — as he calls Oxford, in rivalry with Hall's use of Athens for Cambridge. VII, 25, 158. Diogenes (SV. III, 47) and frequently Socrates (as IX, 119) are accused. For a doubtful reference to masturbation, see III, 52.

native shame".[46] The theatre is mentioned a couple of times as furnishing opportunities for immorality.[47] The mention of sexual disease is of course frequent.[48] Aphrodisiacs are cited, such as oysters, marrow pie, eringoes, sweet potatoes, crab and buttered lobster,[49] while their opposites — camphire, lettuce and thistles — he obtains, characteristically, from Hall.[50] Perverted marriages are only alluded to,[51] not coming strictly within the scope of his satire. Effeminacy[52] is touched upon but lightly. But Marston hates those who have fallen into subjection to women; Hercules as Omphale's servant is a type of the state which his plays often flout.[53]

Hypocrisy is the real theme of the first two satires, and attacks on it are scattered through the others, in many different forms.[54] Thus Tubrio, the soldier, appears brave, but is so only in the wars of the stews,[55] and the covertly sensual man is elsewhere described as "but a muck-hill overspread with snow".[56] His chief assault is upon parasites, which word he, in common with other Elizabethan satirists, uses almost interchangeably with hypocrite. He contrives to make few merely

---

[46] SV. IX, 125. Foreign vices are esp. mentioned S. ii, 127f. Bruto, the traveller, is in some respects an early example of the Malcontent type; — dressed in sad colors, he exclaims against the corrupted age, while he himself went abroad to seek evil. The resemblance to Shakespeare's Jaques is striking. May not Bruto and Jaques both have been drawn from some actual London figure?

Other foreign references are S. iii, 70; SV. IX, 90, with which cf. Hall, III, i. For other contemporary portraits of travellers, see references in Baskerville, p. 271f.

[47] SV. In Lect. 45; IX, 121.

[48] E. g., SV. I, 56; S. ii, 150; S. V., III, 91; VII, 100f.

[49] SV. II, 36; III, 69.

[50] SV. III, 69; Virgid. IV, iv, 109. Cf. also Virgid. IV, i, 122; Ovid, Ars Am., II, 415; Dutch Courtezan, IV, iii, 35.

[51] SV. I, 32; IV, 105; Pr. Lib. II, ad Rhyth., 20; V, 59. For selling of wives, see references to adultery, supra.

[52] S. ii, 125; Pyg., Aut. in Praise, 24. Effeminate is used in the different sense of lustful, SV. VII, 34; cf. Ins. Coun. I, i, 60, and contrast Malc. III, i, 28.

[53] SV. VII, 32.

[54] S. i, Ruscus, and Castilio (cf. infra, p. 108). S. ii, Hall is included under hypocrites, because his satires only pretend to do good, but are too obscure. SV. III, 151; VII, 143f.; S. i, 73; SV. III, 127.

[55] S. i.

[56] SV. VII, 155.

99

typical figures; even when the vice is common, his keen vision separates the figure clearly from the mob, by means of small details which frequently contrive to be highly individual. It would seem to be the rule in his descriptions to have some definite individual in view, and he did not protest so strongly against that supposition as satirists were wont to do.

The Machiavellian is the highest form of parasite,[57] but Marston goes down the list until he reaches Ruscus, who will leave off flattering when he gets some new clothes.[58]

The desire for money is one of the reasons for parasitism; but money with Marston is not nearly so much emphasized as with most of his contemporary satirists. This may have been because Marston himself seems to have been in easy circumstances, but it is extraordinary when the prevalence of English satire on the love of money is noted.[59] Among others[60] he mentions those who (like Falstaff) embezzle war-funds, "bright dirt" as he calls it;[61] and those who owe money, and so make poor ballads out of flattery.[62] Twice he attacks the practise of buying the care of orphan heirs.[63] Usurers are seldom mentioned, but his harshest whipping is given to a

[57] S. ii, 87f.

[58] SV. IV, 57f. S. i, 13. The title of Marston's play *The Fawn* means one who fawns, a use original with him, while its subtitle is the *Parasitaster*.

[59] Hake's *Newes out of Powles* was *Otherwise entituled, syr Nummus. Written in English Satyrs. Wherein is reprooved excessive and unlawful seeking after riches, and the evil spending of the same. (Isham Reprint, 1872.)* The *Steele Glas* satirizes all those who work for gain under the name of peasants. Lodge's first *Satire* deals largely with bribes and usury; his third is addressed "to a deere friend lately given over to covetousnesse", and describes a miser. Hall's Satires II, ii; v; III, i; iii; IV, ii; v; V, ii, iv, are wholly or largely given to this subject.

[60] S. i, 98; SV. IV, 39; V, 95; 20f. Gambling, misers and spendthrifts are given their due; SV. III, 11f.:

"A die, a drab, and filthy broking knaves,
Are the world's wide mouths, all-devouring graves."

See also for gambling, SV. III, 108; IV, 92; XI, 84. Misers, beginning of SV. III. Monopolies, SV., IV, 83; VII, 33; XI, 137.

[61] SV. IV, 2.

[62] Ib. 9. Cf. Hall, I, i, 11f.

[63] SV. II, 58-68; III, 157.

certain Puritan usurer with whom he ruefully acknowledges
to have had dealings:

> "With his bait of purity
> He bit me sore in deepest usurery.
> No Jew, no Turk, would use a Christian
> So inhumanely as this Puritan.
> Diomedes' jades were not so bestial
> As this same seeming-saint, — vile cannibal!" [64]

Here he passes from satire concerning money to that of
Puritanism. Religion was no safe ground for careless satire,
and Marston is exceedingly circumspect in dealing with this
subject. The state of the Church needed reproof as much
perhaps as anything in the age, but reprovers were not popular,
and ecclesiastics had long arms, — and were the censors of the
press. Apart from a few side hits, as at indifference and
simony,[65] there is no mention of the Establishment. But with
dissent he had a free ground. To the satire of the Puritan
usurer he added a long and aptly expressed passage on his
religion, typical of the drama's satire of Puritans:

> "That same devout meal-mouth'd precisian,
> That cries 'Good brother', 'Kind sister', makes a duck
> After the antique grace, can always pluck
> A sacred book out of his civil hose,
> And at the opening and at our stomach's close
> Says with a turned-up eye a solemn grace
> Of half an hour; then with a silken face
> Smiles on the holy crew, and then doth cry,
> 'O manners! O times of impurity!'
> What that depaints a church-reformed state, —
> The which the female tongues magnificate.
>   . . . Who thinks that this good man
> Is a vile, sober, damned politician? . . .
> Who all confusion to the world would bring
> Under the form of their new discipline;
>   . . . to set endless contentious strife
> Betwixt Jehovah and his sacred wife!" [66]

---

[64] S. ii, 71. A clergyman is also attacked, SV. V, 64. See also SV.
I, 25; IV, 73.
[65] SV. III, 133; 151; IV, 31; 39; V, 64.
[66] I. e., the church. S. ii, 58. Cf. *Every Man Out*, Asper on
Puritans, Prol. 39-46.

Elsewhere he says that the 'lewd' precisians scorn church-rites; being forced to take the sacrament, they

> "take the symbol up
> As slovenly as careless courtiers slup
> Their mutton-gruel." [67]

Besides the Puritans, the Roman Catholics were his other permitted prey; rather tediously he shows that he shared the prevailing detestation of them.[68]

He intimates that murder is common, especially inside families; but this is probably a reflection of classic or Italian conditions.[69]

HUMOURS [70]

In the first few satires, humours are clearly divided from other faults. The distinguishing characteristic of a humour is that it is a comparatively small habit or hobby which has warped a man's whole life, until it appears in everything he does. Humours are distinguished from real offences against morals, such as lust, by their comparative harmlessness, yet they engross a man's whole attention. They tend to make him appear ridiculous rather than detestable. So SV. XI, whose title is *Humours,* begins:

> "Sleep, grim Reproof; my *jocund* muse doth *sing*
> In other keys, to nimbler fingering.
> Dull-sprighted *Melancholy,* leave my brain —
> To hell, *Cimmerian night!* in lively vein
> I strive to paint, then hence all *dark* intent
> And sullen frowns! *Come, sport*ing Merriment,
> *Cheek-dimpling* Laughter, crown my very soul
> With jouisance, whilst *mirth*ful jests control
> The gouty humours of these pride-swoll'n days
> . . . I shall break my *sides* at vanity." [71]

[67] SV. II, 94. Other references to Puritans: SV. II, 13; IX, 109f.

[68] *Pyg., Aut in Praise,* 37; SV. III, 58, 65; VIII, 83. Alden has noted the singular way in which Marston often abuses the morals of the classic pantheon (p. 138).

[69] SV. II, 114-128; III, 133. Cf. Juvenal, Sat. III, 116-7.

Lying and blasphemy are mentioned, SV. III, 81; V, 45, VII, 116. Gallus swears "with whole-culverin, raging oaths, to tear the vault of heaven", etc., IV, 21.

[70] Perhaps best dealt with in Baskerville, Chap. III.

[71] Besides the correspondence of theme, the italicised words occur near the beginning of *L'Allegro;* there would seem to be many similarities for mere coincidence.

Thus, one of the objects of Marston's ridicule is Curio, who was always dancing in the street; in characteristic language he says of him:

> "His very soul, his intellectual,
> Is nothing but a mincing capreal." [72]

Luscus can think of nothing but the theatre, and can speak

> "Naught but pure Juliet and Romeo.
> Say who acts best? Drusus or Roscio? . . .
> He writes, he rails, he jests, he courts — what not? —
> And all from out his huge long-scraped stock
> Of well-penned plays." [73]

There are quite a number of other pure humours,[74] most of which seem to us either quite unreal, or simply the result of a man's being wrapt up in his profession. Here lust is plainly outside the ordinary meaning of the term humours, follies to be laughed away; but Marston cannot forbear introducing the subject, the connection being that a man is shown who gives himself up entirely to it.[75] At the end of the satires[76] he still more enlarges the term, by a long warning against submitting to humours, including in them all errors.

The humour most exactly the opposite to Marston's own is that of romantic and formal love-making, which had spread over courtly Europe at the time. Marston was a gentleman, but like Swift he could not have been an especially polite one.

[72] S. i, 125; expanded in SV. XI, 15. *Capreal* is used twice in Davies' *Orchestra*, a poem to which Marston directly after alludes by name. *Intellectual* and *mincing capreal* are quoted by Jonson in *Every Man Out* (see *supra*, p. 133).

[73] S. i, 132. This reference to Shakespeare's play is one of the best evidences of its popularity. Cf. *Insat. Count.* I, i, 195. *Drusus* has been identified with Shakespeare, *Roscius* with Alleyn (Gerald Massey, *Secret Drama of Shakespeare's Sonnets Unfolded*, 1872, pp. 520-3; Grosart, *Introd.* to *Marston's Poems;* Alden, p. 134). There are no sufficient grounds for argument one way or the other; Marston simply meant by the names to indicate well-known actors. Alleyn might probably be in his mind, Shakespeare improbably. Massey's argument that Luscus himself is meant for Shakespeare the plagiarist is absurd. Cf. with this, Pistol's humour.

[74] S. i, 129; 131 and SV. XI, 52; SV. XI passim.

[75] SV. XI, 135f.

[76] Here occurs a single reference to gluttony, where he really has lust in mind.

He hated formalities of every kind; he hated hypocrisy; he despised women as a class: altogether nothing could have been more hateful to him than love-making of the regularized and excessively conventional type which Jonson was to parody in *Cynthia's Revels*.[77] Again and again in his plays is this affectation of the age ridiculed, and the satires contain fierce attacks upon it.

His most complete picture of the inamorate fool is of Lucian, who is sick abed for love, in a chamber hung round with elegies and sonnets, its window-glass full of scratched love-knots. He 'perfumes his mistress with sweet epithets', "Then with a melting look he writhes his head, . . . cries, 'O cruel fair",[78] Shall such a being, who knows no more language than "Sweet lady, kind heart, fair mistress!" and who has never read further than his mistress' lips dare to criticise satires? Again, the monkey of Curio's mistress is dead: it is his duty to attend the funeral and compose mournful elegies. Publius is quite beside himself with joy if he gets possession of one of her hairpins, raving:

> "Celestial bliss,
> Can heaven grant so rich a grace as this?
> Touch it not (by the Lord, sir!) 'tis divine!
> It once beheld her radiant eyes' bright shine;
> Her hair embraced it!"[79]

Marston bittery attacks various lovers' wishes for metamorphoses.[80]

[77] Marston attacks *Cynthia's Revels* more because of the manner than the object of the play.

Cf. Jaques in *As You Like It,* II, vii, 147: "The lover sighing like a furnace, with a woeful ballad made to his mistress' eyebrow." Note how in Shakespeare the satire is kept strictly impersonal.

Marston made fun of his own *Pyg.*, where, he says (S. ii, 1), he himself "lisp'd like an amorist".

[78] In orig., fear; (cf. Hall, I, vii).

[79] S. iii, 55; SV. *In Lect.* 15; SV. VIII (entitled *Inamorato, Curio*).

[80] SV. VIII, 122; wish to be mistress' dog; cf. Lodge, *Fig for Momus, Epist. VI.* Line 126: wish to be wine she drank, or her necklace; cf. Barnes' *Parthenophil, Son.* 63. Line 146: wish to turn hermaphrodite; cf. ibid., *Madrigal* 13. Compare generally Watson's *Hecatompathia.* In 28, from Ronsard, the lover wishes he were a fly, perfume, or a fountain; in 23, he wishes he were a mirror. There are scores of such wishes in literature: e. g., Anacreon, *Odes* XXIII, LXXVII (Moore's translation). *Cf. infra*, p. 110, n.

The new civilization of the Italian Renaissance had been penetrating England ever since the time of Ascham; but luxury was still so novel that it was a staple source of abuse for the satirists of the close of the sixteenth century. The principal method for the display of luxury, then as now, was by means of clothes; satire had a fit mark in the dandy of the time who

> "walks all open-breasted,
> Drawn through the ear with ribands,[81] plumy-crested —
> He that doth snort in fat-fed luxury."[82]

In fact, Marston does not attack many other outlets of the new craze for display.[83]

The male costume of the time gave a splendid opportunity for satire. Most stuffs and colors were exceedingly expensive, coming as they did by hazardous trade-routes, and men vied with one another for display, ordinarily quite out-doing the stiff and ugly apparel of women. The fashions changed with startling frequency, and only varied from one mode of exaggeration to another still more outrageous.[84] Thus Marston describes a youth who has taken two years to get his display together: his ruff

> "hath more doubles far than Ajax' shield . . .
> Under that fair ruff so sprucely set
> Appears a fall, a falling-band forsooth.
> O dapper, rare, complete, sweet nitty[85] youth!
> Jesu Maria! how his clothes appear.
> Crossed and recrossed with lace . . .
> His hat — himself: small crown and huge great brim,
> Fair outward show, and little wit within;
> And all the band with feathers he doth fill,
> Which is the sign of a fantastic still . . .
> His clothes perfumed, his fusty mouth is aired,
> His chin new-swept, his very cheeks are glaired."[86]

[81] Cf. SV. *In Lect.* 32; *W. Y. W.* IV, i, 80; *Ev. Man Out*, II, i.
[82] SV. VII, 30.
[83] A few seem to have classic sources: SV. III, 143, baths of milk and rose-juice; II, 124, precious metals for base vessels, cf. Martial, I, 37.
[84] Cf. Fungoso's chase of fashion in *Ev. Man Out.* The best account of Eliz. fashions is in *Shakespeare's England*, ch. XIX.
[85] Neat [Bullen]
[86] I. e., glazed, with white of egg. [Bullen.] S. iii.

The falling-band, which hung down over the shoulders, under the ruff, was new at the time, and attracted Marston's particular attention. In the first *Satire*, Tubrio's ostrich feather waves gallantly, while his falling-bands of twenty ruffles of Venetian lace, under which he swims along, "doth make him wondrous brave". Another is nothing but a fashion-monger:

> "All fashions, since the first year of this queen,
> May in his study fairly drawn be seen" —[87]

which would mean that he would have a very sizable picture-gallery. It was he who originated the fashions of the long fool's-coat, the huge slop or breeches, and the lugged or eared, boot. A tissue, or lace, slop is mentioned.[88] A religious hypocrite

> "demurely goes
> Right neatly tripping on his new-blacked toes." [89]

Compared to the comment on men's dress, women get little, and that usually in connection with 'surphuled' or painted faces. There is one elaborate portrait of a lady, who comes up in a coach with armorial bearings; at first she wears a mask, but even when she takes that off she is still vizarded:

> "So steeped in lemons' juice, so surpheled,
> I cannot see her face."

She wears a loose gown, with a long slit sleeve, stiff busk, puff farthingale, and a bright-spangled crown. Her ruff makes her appear winged, angelic, but

> "Alas, her soul struts round about her neck;
> Her seat of sense is her rebato[90] set."[91]

But in his satires as elsewhere, it is evident that Marston was more interested in men than in women. It is for this reason that his dealings with them turn mostly on the matter of lust.

[87] SV. XI, 156.
[88] SV. VII, 143.
[89] SV. IV, 40.
[90] Ruff.
[91] SV. VII, 170. See also S. ii, 144; SV. VIII, 8.

The fashion of tabacco seems, from some references in the plays,[92] to have been distasteful to Marston, but it is only mentioned neutrally in the satires;[93] and there are but few references to drunkenness, which habit he asserts is imported from the Low Countries.[94]

CLASSES

Courtiers and gallants seem to take up too great a part, not only in Elizabethan satire, but in the drama also. We have to reckon, not only with the critical theory based on Aristotle's dictum of 'greatness' for the subject, but also with the comparative importance of the court. In mere numbers it was a large establishment, and with its various dependencies it formed a considerable fraction of the population of London. Moreover, in it and dependent noblemen's houses was centered the country's intellectual life, now that the culture of the clergy was at a low ebb. It was a little world of its own, with its own customs, which the rest of England followed afar off. Moreover, it was the great center of spending; it produced nothing and expended much. Being a leisured community, and the most cultured of the country, all innovations, luxuries, and their attendant virtues and vices were necessarily prevalent, the observed of all observers.

Remarkable unanimity prevailed in literature as to the moral atmosphere of a court. The sovereign around which it centered might be either good or bad; but the court as a whole was invariably evil. This comes out most clearly in Fletcher's comedies, but he was only adopting the general convention. There would be one or two wise councillors, a brave and virtuous young courtier (to provide the hero), and a model young lady, preferably a ward (to provide the heroine). The rest of the court were all dissolute, cowardly, hypocritical,

[92] *A. M.*, I, i, 125; III, ii, 74; 281; V, i, 141; *D. C.*, III, iii, 55; *Fawn*, IV, 1, 5; V, i, 361.

[93] SV. *In Lect.*, 11; IX, 77. See also his *Entertainment* (Bullen, III, 399: "Charm hence . . . beards and great tobacco-takers." Other references in Eliz. satire: Hall, *Virgid.*, IV, iv, 40; V, ii, 73; Donne, *Sat.* I; Parkes, *The Curtain Drawer*, 1612, *The World to her Children*, p. 4; K. Bastard's *Chrestoleros*, 1598, Lib. VI, Ep. 19. Other references, Schulze's Hall, *Satiren*, p. 228.

[94] S. ii, 153; cf. SV. III, 142; SV. VII, 107; 124.

false. When a courtier or a court lady is mentioned, we immediately expect a villain, and are rarely disappointed. In all
probability the court, filled with idle rich and those struggling
to get rich quickly without work, pretty well deserved its
reputation.

At any rate, Marston took this view without any hesitation.
He gives a picture of the complete courtier in his first Satire.
His Castilio is probably named from Castiglione, who had
written that book of palace etiquette, the *Courtier*.[95] Castilio
is the model courtier : he can trot a horse in a perfectly harmless tourney ; he can invent devices and mottoes for his shield ;
he can rhyme, ogle, flirt, compliment ; he is famous for revel-
lings and other men's wit.[96] He looks fair and intends foul.
With other courtiers he haunts the citizen's shops, drawn there
by their fair mistresses. With this useless effeminate taking
the place rightfully due a brave warrior, 'Alack ! what hope
for Albion ?" [97]

Gallants are of the same kidney, though they may not be
of such high rank, or frequenters of court, and may be coarse
rather than effeminate. Their qualifications are to have a
good suit, to be in debt and patronize brokers, to keep whores,
swear, swagger and smoke, and use false dice.[98] Gallants are
the special class to which Marston addressed his satires ; he
specifically speaks to them at the end.[99]

The lower classes never had much sympathy from Marston,
nor from most other dramatists. His favorite appellation
for them was 'dunghill peasants',[100] but he did not object to
the variant dungscum rabble, or on occasion mechanic slave
and tinkering knave.[101] He was bitter at the thought of hav-

[95] Marston uses the name Castilio Balthazar for the same type in
A. M. Guilpin in *Skialetheia* uses Castilio and Balthazar. Baskerville
shows how Brisk and Puntarvolo and the satire of *Cynthia's Revels*
are related with this type and this passage of Marston ; p. 22, note ;
190-6.

[96] Oddly, he does not practise music ; but Briscus, who in this passage does, was later utilized by Jonson as Fastidious Brisk in *Every
Man Out*. See Baskerville, p. 191f.

[97] See SV, VIII, 59f., 72f.

[98] SV. IX, 72.

[99] XI, 187, 204.

[100] SV. *In Lect.*, 2 ; IV, 17. He obtained this term from Hall, *Virgid.*
III, i, 78 ; IV, v, 97.

[101] SV. *In Lect.;* X, 14.

ing to write for any but the choice few.[102] But he does commend the people in exactly one instance, where he bewails the common system of short-term tenancy, and asserts that it has killed the strength of England's yeomanry.[103] As Hall said of the malcontent, he was ready enough to praise a thing once it was dead.

Professional men get off rather easily. The old jokes are cracked on doctors: one practitioner killed more men last autumn with hellebore, than the number of the year.[104] Marston's attitude toward the bar is interesting, as his father was a lawyer, and he himself tried law-studies for a time. He mentions new-come law-students a couple of times;[105] and we seem to see reflection of his own difficulties with legal vocabulary, in the part of the law he chooses really to satirize — its barbarous language.[106] Lawyers in general love delays, and are

> "vile necessary evils,
> Smooth-seeming saints, yet damned incarnate devils."

Women play a very slight part in the satires; Marston was not yet expressing (perhaps not yet feeling) his later abundant contempt for them. But it is easy to see his general estimate, in almost his first lines; Pygmalion had avoided women, "knowing their wants and man's perfection."[107]

LITERATURE

It is with this division that Marston began his satiric work for he first of all satirized his own *Pygmalion,* under the pretence that he had not meant it seriously.[108] After this start,

[102] SV. X, 14; IV, 17.
[103] SV. II, 139. Another somewhat vague passage may be sympathetic with the hard-working lot of the tenant-farmer. In it he addresses "sad civility"; N. E. D. quotes the passage as the only illustration of "civility" meaning "a community of citizens collectively."
[104] SV. I, 5; 47; 44.
[105] SV. In Lect. 7; 77.
[106] SV. VII, 81-99.
[107] *Pyg.,* Stan. 1.
[108] *Auth. in Praise;* S. ii, 1, 11; SV. VI, 7 (cf. Persius, Sat. I, 2f.), 60, 65, 89; X, 37.

109

as would be expected he was not backward in attacking contemporary literature — excepting always that which had been attacked by Hall. When the satires were written, Hall was Marston's chief literary enemy, and he devotes much space to attack both on the *Virgidemiarum* and on Hall's personal life.[109]

That Marston knew nothing of Donne's *Satires* is proved by the fact that Marston did not refute Hall's claims to priority. There are few similarities between the satires of Marston and Donne, and those do not show evidence of imitation.[110]

Guilpin's *Skialetheia* was published the same year as the *Satires,* and evidently was written with a knowledge of them. Marston dedicated his *Satira Nova* to Guilpin, and as a friend

---

[109] See *ante*, p. 11f. and Appendix A, Marston's treatment of Hall in the Satires.

[110] Donne, II, 45f.; a lover "woos in language of the Pleas and Courts," as Martius does in terms of fencing, and Luscus in terms of the theatre, SV. XI, 52, 49. Donne, I, 86: his embodied Humour is urged not to dance in the street; as Curio is rebuked for doing, S. i, 124.

One of Marston's lovers desires to be a flea (SV. VIII, 130); Bullen observes that the conceit is out of the ordinary, and wonders if Donne's poem, *A Flea in his Mistress' Bosom,* had been already written. A comic poem, *The Flea-hunt,* was already well known in German literature; and the same idea had been expressed at least three times previously in English. The Clown in *Dr. Faustus* utters the wish, Sc. iv, and in Sc. vi Pride says, "I am like Ovid's flea, etc.", alluding to the mediaeval *Carmen de Pulice,* ascribed to Ovid. Matthew Grove, in his *History of Pelops,* 1587, under *The Restless Estate of a Lover* (p. 68, Grosart *Reprint*), desires to be, among other things, 'a pretty little hound on her with faithful heart to fawn', a chirping mouse, a linnet in a wretched cage, a Philip Sparrow on her fist, and finally

> "A little Robin that doth hop
> about with reddish breast
> Or else if Jove would me convert
> a black flea in her nest."

Thus there is no occasion to refer the conceit to Donne. It was again expressed in *Pasquil's Nightcap,* 1612 (1. 1219).

might well have seen *Skialetheia* before its publication, but there is little connection between the two pieces of work.[111]

Lodge was attacked, justly, for writing as a foolish amorist. His first satire was on hypocrisy, as were the first satires in both of Marston's volumes; it was, however, a common subject for satirists. Barnes is attacked for an amorous wish in his *Parthenophil*, a wish of the sort that would particularly attract Marston's attention.

In S. i, 120, Marston bids the lewd soldier Tubrio unmask, and show Dametus' face; Dametus, as Bullen notes, was the foolish shepherd in Sidney's *Arcadia*. There are two allusions to Spenser.[112]

Besides these, there are a considerable number of references to unrecognizable (or perhaps imaginary) poets. He attacks lacivious and amorous poets, such as the writer of 'Sixty sonnets on kissing his Laura's picture'.[113] One would think that Marston of all men had no reason to make fun of the vocabulary of others, at least for using unusual words, but

---

[111] Bullen noticed a couple of similarities (S. i, 26; SV. VII, 167). J. P. Collier, *Introd.* to *Skialetheia*, (*Miscel. Tracts*), states that "Marston is ridiculed as Fuscus", but this is guesswork. Guilpin's first Epigram, *Procemium*, says that English wits, having overcome barbarism,
> "with self-wounding spite
> Engrave themselves in civil wars' abysms,
> Seeking by all means to destroy each other;"

Therefore we would expect to hear more or less of the literary quarrels of the day. *Ep.* 8, To Deloney, ends:
> "At every street's end Fuscus' rhymes are read.
> And thine in silence must be buried";

and *Ep.* 19 says that an admirer says Fuscus's rhymes instead of grace at meals. This is a small foundation for a theory. With *Ep.* 46, *On the Viol de Gambo*, cf. S. i, 21. Guilpin's *Satire* 5, p. 50, calls a gallant: "The exact pattern which Castilio Took for's accomplished courtier;" this is evidence that Marston's Castilio was certainly taken from Castiglione. For Guilpin's mention of *Reactio*, see *supra*, p. 14. There are a couple of passages connected with other plays: *Ep.* 68 speaks of "the Irishmen crying 'Pip, fine pip' with a shrill accent", as in *Old Fortunatus*. Chester, the original of Carlo Buffone, is referred to, *Satire Preludium*, p. 27, and *Sat.* I, p. 35.

[112] SV. VI, 36, 59.

[113] SV. VIII, 141; XI, 146.

he did not hesitate.[114] He himself borrows occasionally quite freely, but nevertheless he attacks plagiarism even more freely.[115]

Various poets are satirized in SV. VI, but most of the references are so vague as to make identification very hazardous. One has to invoke some drab before he can write; Marston might well have been thinking of his own verses prefatory to *Pygmalion,* entitled *To his Mistress,* which he elsewhere asserts, however, to have been written as a satire on their kind.[116] Another poet has produced "a prodigy, some monstrous misshapen balladry", probably one of the long histories in verse such as the *Mortimeriados* or the *Mirror for Magistrates* which he elsewhere defends.

A poet while out walking lies down, and falling asleep dreams of fairies and a flowery vale. Winckler[117] suggests Thomas Edwards, the author of *Cephalus and Procris,* but the correspondence is too slight, the heroine only meeting an elf in the woods. Grosart somewhat more plausibly suggests John Dickenson, the publisher of a collection of verse, *The Shepherd's Complaint,* 1594; or Drayton. Neither fits the situation very well, however.

It is of little use to try to identify the poet whose strains were so high that his poetry collapsed; or the poet who to get a reputation for learning wrote fustian in unintelligible words. Winckler proposed for the latter the anonymous author of *Zepheria,* 1594, but the use of foreign words such as is found there is not what Marston seems to be referring to. Likewise the poet who made Homer cite Spenser has not been discovered—if indeed he ever existed.

Critics are thoroughly overhauled[118]—rich and poor, young and old, courtier and artizan are scorned in this first of Marston's work, before they had had a chance to criticise him. Their reproof, he says, only makes him 'bristle up his plumes of pride'. He does allow, in conclusion, that there exist some diviner spirits who by reading his work will not

[114] SV. *To Perusers,* 15; VI, 48, 55.
[115] S. i, 46; ii, 47; SV. XI, 77; *Entertainment,* p. 399. Cf. SV. VI, 59.
[116] *Auth. in Praise,* 11.
[117] P. 37.
[118] In his address *In Lectores* before his *S. of V.*

disgrace him. After another passage[119] chastising critics, he ends, "He that thinks worse of my rhymes than myself, I scorn him, for he cannot; he that thinks better, is a fool . . . If thou perusest me with an impartial eye, read on; if otherwise, know I neither value thee nor thy censure." Were this to be taken literally, one fails to see why he should object to his critics, save on the general principle that he objected to nearly everyone; but of course the sentiment is simply the conventional expression of the malcontent satirist.

That he did care much for what was said of him is shown by the devotion of most of a satire—the sixth—to the critics of his *Pygmalion*. In connection with the passage just quoted, it is interesting to read the conclusion of this satire:

> "What though the sacred issue of my soul
> I here expose to idiots' control;
> What though I bare to lewd opinion,
> Lay ope to vulgar profanation,
> My very genius, etc."

No one could take his work more seriously.

In general Marston is a good literary critic, as is evident in some of his prefaces. In these early satires, where Hall is not concerned he shows himself fair, so far as we can judge, and usually interesting; but so much cannot be said for his savage censures of Hall, and these form much the greater part of his literary satire. Aside from a few clever hits at real absurdities, they seem inspired by hatred, envy and malice, for which we can find no just cause.

SOURCES

The English formal satire existed because of imitation of the Roman satirists. From them were drawn its form, its style, its obscurity, its use of proper names, and, more important, much if not most of its subject-matter. Most of the Elizabethan satirists abused this natural dependence; Hall, Donne and Lodge, for instance, besides using general classical settings and incidents,[120] translated whole short satires directly from the Romans, without acknowledgment.

[119] To those that seem judicial Perusers.
[120] supra, p. 85.

Among them Marston was singularly independent. He adopted the general form, the proper names, and on some special occasions the obscure style which was theoretically the proper dress for satire. Hall's satires were his starting point, and his work can frequently be referred to them, but he opposes rather than imitates. No wholesale borrowing is to be found in Marston's satires, and careful search is necessary for even minor instances of imitation of the classics.[121]

His bent toward lust and his inclusion of bestial crimes, would, one naturally supposes, have sent him to Juvenal and Persius for inspiration; yet he has availed himself of them but slightly. Martial is of all classic poets most akin to an important phase of Marston's work,—the depiction of instances of lust in telling phrases. There are enough references to make us sure that he was acquainted with Martial's epigrams; but we find almost no copying of Martial's ideas.

Grosart says, "Speaking generally of his *Satires,* Persius rather than Juvenal is followed. This is seen in the cryptic obscurity of *Reactio."*[122] Marston himself speaks of both as being obscure,[123] and as a matter of fact, he seems to have made more references to Juvenal than to any other classical source. On the whole, English satire seems to have received more of its guiding impulse from Juvenal than from any other source. Hall owed his inspiration and considerable material to Juvenal, his tone to Seneca. He was followed by Marston save in the matter of direct borrowing from the classics. Nowhere has Marston utilized the classics for more than isolated details; and he knew no other English satire save Hall's.

His true sources were his own observation and imagination, and (as his foe, the *Whipper of the Satire,* alleged) the rumors of the streets, and the devil. His borrowings from the classics are so trivial that I have felt it possible merely to indicate them in an appendix.[124] When the strength of the

[121] He ridicules a critic who pretends to find classic sources for his "respectless, free-hand poesy." SV. VI, 93.

[122] Introd. to *Poems of Marston,* p. liii.

[123] In his prefatory address to *Judicial Perusers.*

[124] A list of allusions and quotations from the classics is given in Appendix E.

influence under which he worked is considered, he must be credited with a remarkable degree of originality.

Marston's use of proper names is more conventional. English satirists early adopted the habit of using classic pseudonyms for the objects of their satire. Gascoigne began the practise by introducing two traditional type-names, Lucrece and Lais. Classical names were used freely for the first time by Donne, followed by Lodge, Hall and Guilpin. About nine-tenths of the names used by Marston are classical. In few cases did he preserve the characteristics which classical satirists had attached to the names, save with several which he used as Hall had done.[125]

GENERAL ESTIMATE

Among the productions of the school of Elizabethan satirists, Marston's satires may safely be ranked third. In interest they are surpassed by Hall's, and in literary ability by Donne's; but to all others of the period they are distinctly superior.

These satires came at the height of a passing phase of Elizabethan activity. Satire succeeded the vogue of the sonnet in lyric poetry, the supremacy of romantic comedy in drama. It ushered in the more serious Jacobean poetry of Sylvester, Davies, the Fletchers, Brown, Wither—the school of Spenser and the tribe of Ben; in the drama, it immediately preceded the dominance of tragedy and tragic-comedy. It thus formed a transition from one era to another.

Again, together with the work of Jonson the satire began a temporary reaction of the classic influence. The humanists had ruled the first two-thirds of the century; but with the passing of such men as Sydney and Harvey, they ceased to exert primary influence. The dominant late Elizabethan note is romantic. At the end of the century, however, classicism led by Ben Jonson made another struggle for supremacy. It was not to succeed, in poetry or drama, till after the Revolution; nevertheless its attempt at this time left its impress on all literature. It is easily to be discerned, for instance, in the prose style of Bacon and Hall. In poetry, the dominant mode was satiric, and this was directly inspired and guided

---

[125] See second part of Appendix E.

by classic models. The Epigram and Character show satiric prose also influenced by the classics.

What caused the sudden outburst of satire at the end of the sixteenth century? It is difficult to explain satisfactorily any such literary movement. The other great age for English satire was during the latter part of the seventeenth and the beginning of the eighteenth century, and was in essence a return toward Puritanism, after the licence of the Restoration.[126] It may be that some such cause produced the Elizabethan satire also.

There can be no doubt that the Reformation in England dealt tremendous blows, at least temporarily, to popular religion. The repeated alternations of the state form of religion under the different Tudor monarchs ended by producing passionate partizanship to particular views in the few, and considerable indifference to religion in the many. The clergy, deprived of all foreign support and the prestige of an universal church organization, became almost powerless, and dependent as never before on patronage for existence, until such a state of servitude as is pictured in the second *Return from Parnassus,* for instance, could become not unusual.

With the decline of religious influence, there happened to come into England more luxury. Rapid growth in wealth and, after the defeat of the Armada, an increasing feeling of security, tended to complete the work of the Renaissance. Furthermore, all society was taking its tone from Italian manners and books. Puritanism was already beginning to leaven the lump of English materialism, but its influence was not yet powerful enough to change the outward, much less the inward tone of society.

The effects of this increasing culture and decreasing religious control were shown vividly in the usual ways; dress, literature, the drama, and sexual relations were all showing extravagances and excesses. These it were which brought on the attacks of the satirists, because the less and less restrained excesses were visible to all men.

Thus it is not so entirely strange that a young literary man beginning his profession in the closing years of the sixteenth century should have been affected by both trends of feeling:

[126] *Hudibras* belongs rather to the earlier age of Restoration controversy.

that in the same year he should both write lascivious poetry, and also write against writing it But it required the odd personal twist of a Marston to publish both pieces of work in the same book. His formal satires were all written before Marston was 25, and too much should not be expected from them. But having begun thus, he continued the practice, though somewhat less openly, all through his literary career. There is not one of his plays which does not contain some plain bawdry, and most contain much; but he invariably assumes that by it he is serving a moral purpose. In this, so complex is human character, he may well have been sincere.

Satire suited Marston's critical, mordant spirit. Yet we seldom feel that he is giving all his heart to it. No matter how much he protests, now and again we detect a hollow ring in his speech. This is true also of the lust of *Pygmalion* —like his marble statue, form is there, but no life, nor is that life ever breathed into it. Marston was not really moved by what he was writing, and neither is the reader. The interest is intellectual, not emotional; one has ever the feeling of a literary exercise. The same thing is true of Marston's dramatic work. This, I believe, is the main reason why Marston ranks as low as he does, notwithstanding his considerable gifts of expression. It is only now and then that one feels the author's emotion behind the printed page—in the denunciation of the Puritan usurer, for instance, or in the depiction of Franceschina in the *Dutch Courtezan*.

It results that no commentator has been able to believe that Marston was sincere in his denunciation of contemporary society. Thus Warton says, "The satirist who too freely indulges himself in the display of that licentiousness which he means to proscribe, absolutely defeats his own design." Alden,[127] quoting this, observes of Marston: "That he was inspired by any very serious desire of promoting reform, however, it is difficult to believe. He shows an unpleasant satisfaction in dwelling on unclean details." And Bullen says,[128] "Modern readers will feel that Marston was not driven by 'sacva indignatio' to write satires, and they will not be inclined to accept the young author of *Pygmalion* as a sedate

[127] P. 135, *Formal Satire.*
[128] *Marston*, I, xxiii.

117

moralist." Probably his highest praise as a satirist has come from Grosart.[129]

"I am not blind to offences versus good manners and taste, and even worse, in Marston's *Satires*. But I must claim for them — even above Hall's — a fearless, trenchant striking at the highest-seated evildoers . . . I am willing to believe that he wrote from patriotism and conscience. (See his manly lines *To Detraction*, and the grave, solemn close of all, *To Everlasting Oblivion*. Equally throbbing with emotion and vitality of conviction is the final close of the *Proemium in Liber Tertium*.) For putridities of allusion, common to him with the *Virgidemiarum* and Donne and all, there is Henry Parrott's pleading:
'Be not aggrieved my humourous lines afford
Of looser language here and there a word:
Who undertakes to sweep a common sink
I cannot blame him though his besom stink.'"

But it is difficult to believe that the world was for him such a black place as he pictures it in his satires.

It was, however, no temporary pose of Marston; the more one reads his plays, the more one is obliged to admit that at any rate he was always consistent in his low opinion of life. Satire is usually a passing phase. Many men, as Persius, Donne, Hall, have been satirists when they were young, and today the most intemperate criticisms of society and morals are apt to come from undergraduates. But it has not been so with the great satirists: Juvenal is said to have been banished for his satires when an octogenarian; Swift, Pope, the modern Samuel Butler were satirists all their lives. When the history of the satiric element in the Elizabethan Drama comes to be written, it will be found that the proportion of satire in the dramas of Marston is unsurpassed by that of any poet of the age, with the possible exception of Jonson. And it is all the bitter, extreme, rancorous satire of the *Scourge of Villainy*. It is evident that in his first literary work Marston was not pretending to a feeling he did not possess.

Critics have been misled by Marston's own attitude. He openly flouts his own work. In the margin opposite Line 15 of the first satire of the *Scourge of Villainy*, he puts "*Huc usque Xylinum*": Thus far, bombast. At the conclusion of

[129] Introd., p. xx.

his satires he apparently takes off his tragic mask, and shows the face of the jester underneath:

> "Here ends my rage. Though angry brow was bent,
> Yet have I sung in sporting merriment."

Such lines as these cannot but give the idea that the poet had not really meant much of what he had been saying so furiously; that the crack of his satiric whip was but the empty threat of a ring-master.

The satiric spirit was too much a part of Marston, to allow us to take this natural conclusion as the truth. Doubtless he did say more than he meant in his satires; he must have known that the world was not as bad as he was assuming. His conception of the requirements for the role of satirist made him preternaturally severe, and filled his verses with scourgings. His ridicule of himself shows reaction against this abnormal gloom, which was partly his own, partly assumed professionally. But at the bottom Marston was indignant at the world, and contemptuous of it; he had something of what Swinburne apostrophized as his "noble heart of hatred." The true and natural expression of it in his work is hard to find, because in his satires it was overlaid by his makebelieve *schrecklichkeit,* the machinery which he deemed necessary for the formal satire; in his plays expressions of his detestation for vicious environment are discounted by immediately surrounding licentious passages. One must endeavor to judge Marston, not from details, but from his work as a whole.

Taking this wider outlook, I feel sure that Marston regarded himself as being, like his own Malcontent or Fawn, in the world but not of it. He is among enemies; to save himself his true worth is disguised, and he chooses to play the part of fool although he is wiser than those who despise him. He apparently falls in with the schemes and baseness of those about him, since thus he amuses them and so will gain his own ends. In reality he despises them, and, so far as he is obliged to be like them, despises himself also. No doubt he is wiser, he feels, but only in being able to perceive the weaknesses of their natures, and consequently, of his own. This feeling of playing a part, of going in disguise, is what enables him to make fun of his own work, and to appear double-natured, sinning and opposing sin at the same time. This underlying melancholy would bring forth such utterances as his dedication of the satires to oblivion.

Marston himself may be viewed as a Malcontent. Certain characteristics of Hamlet, and portions of Burton's *Anatomy of Melancholy*, are very suggestive of explanations for Marston's life and writings. Most of his critics have been at fault in their conceptions of the man, because he displayed a type of feeling which is foreign to our day; he practised a code well recognized by his contemporaries, but forgotten by us, though we have Hamlet as its perfect exemplar.

The experience might be called one of the growing-pains of the modern world—our world which was born amid the birth pangs and joys of the Renaissance and the Reformation. The unified Christian philosophy of the Middle Ages had to be abandoned, bit by bit, and this could only be achieved through anguish. To thoughtful Elizabethans the earlier simplicity of faith was gone, and there was nothing certain to replace it. To Marston as to Hamlet the world was out of joint. They were between two worlds, one dying, the other powerless to be born, and more truly so than Matthew Arnold. When the results of the theory of evolution began to show Victorians that another saving remnant of the mediaeval faith could not survive, the world had the ideals of liberty, democracy, fraternity or service, and science to take its place. The Elizabethans had no similar ideals, save the dawnings of nationalism and science.

Thinking men fell back upon the libertine and stoic philosophies of the ancients. Both of these are represented in Montaigne, and this may help to explain why his influence was so great with the Elizabethans. These philosophies both are attempts to make the best of an incomprehensible world, and so certain of their elements were acceptable together, but as systems they are ultimately incompatible. The attempt to assimilate both produced the Malcontent type in certain sincere men who lacked the optimism which other causes had engendered in the age. They were at odds with their environment; their philosophy was incoherent; therefore they were at odds with themselves. Marston's mixture of villainy-scourging and ribaldry is but typical.

Most of the condemnation of Marston has been caused by his treatment of lust. *Pygmalion* is perhaps the most frankly sensual—at any rate free-spoken—poem with much pretence to being literature, that the Elizabethan age produced, and it was an age by no means squeamish.[130] Certainly none of his predecessors [131] in this kind of poetry—the amorous narrative with a classical source — were so consistently lascivious; nor were his successors.[132] His satires which followed *Pygmalion* fully carried out this theme. It is not that so great space is given in Marston's satire to lust—though it far exceeds that devoted to any other subject. It is the quality that is especially noticeable,

> "Which, like a Paphian, wantonly displays
> The Salaminian titillations
> Which tickle up our lewd Priapians."

His attitude in this regard is connected with that in another, his treatment of filth. Marston's mind, in this as in many other instances, reminds us of Swift's. Swift, we know, had an almost morbid detestation of dirt in any form, and was himself almost painfully clean; yet his writings, especially some of the poems and his description of the Yahoos, continually present to the reader vivid pictures of filth. It is as though his mind could not escape the subject; he almost gloats on it, when it appears in other, and to him despicable persons, or in humanity as a whole. Marston must have had much of Swift's nature in this regard. He continually employs, for example, such onamatopoeic words as blandishment, lusk, nasty, streaking,[133] surphuled and such-like. The following is a good sample of his verbiage, with its abundant liquids and sibillants and open vowels:

[130] For comparison, one must take such a poem as Nashe's *The Choise of Valentines*, c. 1595.

[131] Cf. *supra*, p. 88, n.

[132] In such works as T. N.'s *Barley-break, or Warning for Wantons*, 1607; Barksted's *Mirrha, Mother of Adonis*, 1607; or his *Hiren the Fair Greek*, 1611; Austin's *Scourge of Venus, or the Wanton Lady*, 1614; or Gresham's *Picture of Incest, or Cinyras and Myrrha*, 1624.

[133] I. e., stretching, as on a bed.

121

"Lust hath confounded all;
The bright gloss of our intellectual
Is foully soiled. The wanton wallowing
In fond delights, and amorous dallying,
Hath dusked the fairest splendor of our soul;
Nothing now left but carcass, loathsome, foul;
For sure, if that some sprite remained still,
Could it be subject to lewd Lais' will?
    . . . Leaving the sensual
Base hangers-on lusking at home in slime,
Such as was wont to stop port Esquiline." [134]

Visions of lust and filth have a fascination for Marston, not only in his satires, where, if anywhere, they might be in place, but also in all his plays; and they are presented forcefully and tellingly. His was no more a normal mind than Swift's; I do not think we can judge one any more than the other solely from his writings. In the case of Swift we have a large number of external accounts, and can get some idea of this, one of the greatest figures of English literature, apart from what he has chosen to set down for us. That is not possible in the case of Marston. We are not able safely to judge of his character. Amazement has been expressed over his entering the church; but needlessly. In the first place, holy orders did not mean then what they do now in regard to strictness of living. Moreover, it seems to me that Marston would have made a better clergyman than Herrick or, later, Sterne. His piety one imagines would have been of the type of Swift's: cold, detesting vice, doing good by stealth rather than openly.

Like Swift, again, Marston was prevailingly intellectual, not emotional. The lust described in *Pygmalion* or anywhere in Marston does not stir us, because we feel that the author himself was cold at the time of composition, without even much recollected passion. He touches certain nerves with the scientific feeling that possesses a surgeon in a dissection. The result is a lack of life, of glow, which in the satires he vainly tried to supply by rhetorical extravagance. This purely intellectual exposure of ugliness tends to disgust us, even as it does in Swift; and Marston does not have the redemption of Swift's genius.

[134] SV. VIII, 165f.

Furthermore, the satires are often obscure. This arises from policy, not lack of ability; in the rest of Marston's work there is almost always clear and most vigorous expression. In the preface of the *Scourge of Villany* he gives his own doctrine in the matter of satiric style. The general view of his day was that one of the requirements of a satire was obscurity,[135] such as that which readers found in Persius. But Persius, Marston says, is hard to read because he is ancient, and because of his references to private customs of his time now forgotten; the same is the case with Juvenal. "Yet both of them go a good seemly pace, not stumbling, shuffling." Even Chaucer, he says, is difficult for us to understand; "but had we then lived, the understanding of them would have been nothing hard. I will not deny, there is a seemly decorum to be observed, and a peculiar kind of speech for a satire's lips," which he can more easily understand than explain. He would, however, have the subject-matter rough, rather than the style. "I cannot, nay, I will not, delude your sight with mists; yet I dare defend my plainness against the verjuice-face of the crabb'st satirist that ever stuttered." To satirize vices in such an obscure way that no man understands you, is foolishness[136] Here we see that Marston had the true doctrine; but he was far from always living up to it. The Elizabethans felt that the Roman satirists were especially hard reading, and this quality was imitated along with the others of their models. Marston correctly understood the reasons for the lack of clearness in the older satires; but he was swayed by his time to the extent of believing in "a peculiar kind of speech for a satire's lips", which peculiarity consisted largely of fustian. It must not be forgotten that the Elizabethans had a good cause for obscurity, because of the necessity for avoiding libel suits and personal quarrels: hence too the many statements of the satirists that they attack no individuals, but only classes.

The Elizabethan satirists are not so obscure as most critics have asserted. Donne's style is of course crabbed, but his meaning is throughout fairly clear. Hall is very regular in

[135] This general attitude of the Eliz. satirists, and the universal modern criticism of their obscurity, is fully dealt with by Alden, *Rise of Formal Satire in England*, pp. 102-8, 131-2.

[136] He is presumably hitting at Hall.

style, though now and then intentionally cloudy in meaning, as, for instance, in the first satire of his fourth book. Marston, in spite of his protestations of clear writing, is the most difficult to read of the three. Sometimes he is intentionally talking in the "peculiar kind of speech".[137] But more frequently the reader's difficulty arises from Marston's extreme concision of style. He packs meanings into short phrases, discards connectives, and indulges freely in interjections. Take for example the account of the sectary who has obtained riches from his followers, but who will conform to the Church of England if his wealth be threatened:

> "When that the strange ideas in his head
> (Broached 'mongst curious sots, by shadows led)
> Have furnish'd him, by his hoar auditors,
> Of fair demesnes and goodly rich manors;
> Sooth, then he will repent when's treasury
> Shall force him to disclaim his heresy.
> What will not poor need force? But, being sped,
> God for us all! the gourmand's paunch is fed;
> His mind is changed."[138]

Of the cheating tradesman, Marston wrote:

> "Now since he hath the grace, thus graceless be,
> His neighbors swear he'll swell with treasury.
> Tut, who maintains such goods, ill-got, decay?
> No, they'll stick by thy soul, they'll ne'er away."[139]

While this conciseness is frequently a fault, it has its other aspect. It gives to Marston's work a rare degree of force and vividness. We may not like what he says, but if we read him at all we cannot disregard him. He is apt at drawing little character-portraits in which no world is lost, and sometimes his couplets have a Pope-like compression:

> "Then Muto comes, with his new glass-set face,
> And with his late-kissed hand my book doth grace,
> Straight reads, then smiles, and lisps, ''Tis pretty good'.
> And praiseth that he never understood."[140]

[137] As in S. iv and v, and SV. Proem. Lib. I, and VI.
[138] SV. IV, 43f.
[139] SV. V, 74.
[140] SV. VI, 77.

124

His style lends especial vehemence to his expression of scorn:

> "Here's one would be his mistress' necklace, fain
> To clip her fair, and kiss her azure vein.
> Fond fools, well wished, and pity but should be:
> For beastly shape to brutish souls agree.
> If Laura's painted lip do deign a kiss
> To her enamoured slave — "O· Heaven's bliss!"
> (Straight he exclaims) "not to be matched with this!"
> Blaspheming dolt! go three-score sonnets write
> Upon a picture's kiss. O raving sprite."[141]

Marston wrote very little poetry that is quotable for its own sake. One would not expect it in satires, whose object is not beauty save negatively, in the scorn of ugliness. But his plays show that he lacks almost entirely the lyric gift of the Elizabethan age. Many of his plays were performed by children's companies, and as a matter of course, contained much singing. It is true there are many stage directions for songs, but very few of the songs themselves are printed, and those are mostly doggerel or scurrilous bits.[142] In the six plays collected in the 1633 volume there are only seven songs printed, and four of them are doggerel. There is an eight line love song, of no especial merit:[143] *Sophonisba* contains a queer, abrupt, infernal song to Erictho:[144] and Quadratus in *What You Will* sings or says an Epicurean poem:

> "Music, tobacco, sack and sleep,
> The tide of sorrow backward keep.
> If thou art sad at others' fate,
> Rivo, drink deep, give care the mate . . .
> Whilst quickest sense doth freshly last,
> Clip time about, hug pleasure fast."[145]

In the one play of *Jack Drum* there are five songs, all of them comic. There is the usurer's

> "Chunck-chunck, chunck-chunck, his bags do ring,
> A merry note with chuncks to sing."

[141] SV. VIII, 138. He probably means that Laura's face is so painted that there is no difference between kissing her and her picture.
[142] Thus, *A. M.*, III, ii, 32; 271; *Mal.* V, ii, 1; *D. C.* I, ii, 120; IV, v, 70; *J. D. E.* I, 53; II, 17; 78.
[143] *D. C.* V, ii, 36.
[144] IV, i, 192.
[145] II, i, 272.

125

Two make an attempt at love poetry,[146] one beginning well:

"Delicious beauty that doth lie
Wrapt in a skin of ivory."

Finally there is a repetitive drinking song of nearly fifty lines, rehearsing the measures of wine.[147] These thirteen songs are all that we have in the plays, and not one of them sustains or more than hints at the true lyric note. Marston was attempting what he could not do. Likewise there are several attempts at fine writing in the plays, but successes are lamentably few. Lamb picked out thirteen passages of varying lengths from Marston's plays.[148] One of these[149] was taken bodily from Sylvester's Du Bartas, and some others may be from as yet unidentified sources, — because Marston was not, from his nature, really poetical. He had a clear vision, which he usually bent downward; and an incisive, graphic way of speaking. His thoughts are constantly jetting out, in exclamations and broken sentences and rhetorical questions;[150] his emotions are almost never tender, or soft, though they are sometimes kindly; even his smiles are bitter. This is not such stuff as lyrics or lyrical passages are made of. Marston was essentially intellectual, and was only rarely and then incompletely dominated by emotion. With his critical faculty and ability for powerful writing, he would have felt much more at home in Augustan than in Elizabethan England.

The chief value of Marston's satires lies in their depiction of the times and of Marston's attitude toward them. With all due allowance for his exaggeration for the sake of effect, much of what he writes he must have observed. For Marston was not a highly imaginative poet, but rather of Ben Jonson's realistic turn of mind. Furthermore, he does not

[146] II, 17 and III, 140.
[147] V, 338.
[148] A. M. III, i, 1-91; A. R. Prol.; III, i, 142-203; II, i, 78-84; IV, ii, 292-310; IV, i, 36-48; I, i, 107-9; Mal. III, i, 157-170; IV, ii, 41-51; Soph. IV, i, 89-123; 144-168; W. Y. W. I, i, 133-155; III, ii, 86-94; II, ii, 151-5; 159-180. These do not include selections from the Insatiate Countess, since proved for the most part not Marston's.
[149] Mal. IV, ii, 41-51.
[150] There are many passages where Marston's blank verse, especially when conversational, by its rapidity and conciseness reminds one of Browning.

seem to have drawn largely for his facts from any discoverable literary source. On the subject of lust he was certainly carried away by the fascination the subject possessed for him, and it is here we feel most strongly the influence of the classic satirists, though he rarely draws his material directly from them. Certainly, if we can judge from the other literature of the time, some of the gross abuses of this kind which he retails were not common faults of his age. Aside from this, his lovers, gallants, usurers, puritans, fops and soldiers are depictions of individuals and classes as they actually existed in London in 1600.

We learn much too about himself, and are aided to a better understanding of his dramas. We find that he was expressing himself in the characters of malcontents, and so we can see how far he is the embodiment of that 'humour' of the time which produced for us the character of Hamlet. He displays his interest in lust, combining strangely fascination and disdain; he shows his deep scorn for weak affected love, and infatuation, which must have been incomprehensible to his cold temperament, save in its Stoic explanation as a form of insanity. Meanwhile his comparative lack of interest in women is evident — he only writes of them as they affect men, and this is to be his consistent method in his plays. Therefore, while Marston's satires cannot be placed in the first or in the second class of literary productions, they are nevertheless valuable from the standpoint of their bearing on contemporary literature, his times and himself.

DRAMATIC SATIRE

We have seen that Marston initiated his literary career by publishing an erotic poem in the same volume with *Certain Satires*. This indicated the path which his plays were to follow, for they all combine these two elements of lust and satire; the proportions may vary, but both are always present. The purpose of the following pages is to indicate the relative amounts and varying aims of the satire in the different plays, and to discover some definite progress or trend in Marston's practice. The kind of satire occurring in each play will be roughly grouped as was done for the formal satires — i. e., under general satire, morals, humours, fashions, classes and literature.

ANTONIO AND MELLIDA

This play may be called a tragi-comedy of intrigue. It was written at about the same time as the *Satires*, 1598-9. Since it was the initial attempt of Marston at drama, the romance is crude, its simplicity sometimes absurd. This makes more evident the discrepancy between the romantic story and the satire, which is the most prominent element of the play.

The young playwright's attitude is one of scorn for the world; and it is by means of scorn that he chiefly endeavors to make his protagonists heroic. He does not do this so much positively (except by a general ascription of the virtues) as negatively, by making their attitude one of disdain for their environment. It is not that they are so good, but that everyone else is so much worse.

This is the attitude of Marston himself in the satire which the play contains. It is dedicated to Nobody,[1] "the only rewarder of virtuous merits, bounteous Mecaenas of poetry and Lord Protector of oppressed innocence". One actor in the Induction says of himself that 'he plays the part of all the world — a fool',[2] and Andrugio concludes that "earthly dirt

[1] For this use of Nobody as a convention of the time, cf. Baskerville, p. 11, n. Something of the same idea may be in the *Dedication* of *SV*. to Oblivion.

[2] Cf. SV. VII, 139, the world drowned in all vileness, and the motto of SV. X, *Stultorum plena sunt omnia*.

makes all things, makes the man, moulds me up honor".[3]   In
most of his plays, Marston introduces a character representing
his own opinions, who usually acts and talks as it may be
supposed Marston himself would have done in like circumstances.   In this play Feliche is the author's representative.
He is the honest courtier who befriends the hero and exposes
foolishness, and whose philosophy is the one current about
1600, stoicism.   He is described at some length in the Induction,[4] as possessing the true stoic content — he never thinks
any man perfect, either in nature or fortune, consequently he
is fitted to judge the world justly, without favoritism because
without envy.   This is of course Marston's real attitude
throughout the satires, though it is never expressed there so
clearly.   Feliche views the world as an evil place, possessing
little more of virtue than the idea.

Under MORALS, the usually prominent place of lust is
taken by flattery, especially as manifested in parasites.   This
vice is embodied in the 'supple-chapt flatterer' Forobosco, who,
as Marston characteristically expresses it, attempts with
"servile patches of glavering flattery to stitch up the bracks
of unworthily honored" gentility.[5]

As would be expected from the date of *Antonio and Mel-*
lida, it comes under the influence of Jonson's humour plays,
and is full of HUMOURS itself.   Indeed, the lengthy Induction is little more than description of the different humours
of the characters, quite in Jonson's style.   Here Feliche, the
author's representative, describes himself, and then turns to
the hero, Antonio, with "But last, good, thy humour?"   These
two, Feliche and Antonio, are the most important characters
in the play, from the author's standpoint, for he promises
their further depiction in a second part.[6]   It was by uniting
these two characters that Marston later framed the *Malcontent.*
Antonio is the hero in misfortune, who intrigues and struggles,

---

[3] III, i, 31; cf. III, ii, 42f.
[4] Lines 108f.
[5] Cf. also the opening of Act III; Feliche in II, i; opening of III,
ii, and l. 164. For satire on pride, see I, i, 45. Money, III, i, 95-100.
The last line has a Marlowian ring. Cf. also mention of money ob-
taining love, V, i, 55. Cf. 98, rightly spoken of the duke by Feliche,
who then exits.
[6] Ind. 150. Not fulfilled. Cf. infra.

and finally vanquishes[7]: Feliche is the man in court who is honest in a world of knaves, and who exposes and ridicules them; he too is secretly scheming for the rightful ruler. It is easy to see why he was not developed in the second part, as the first had promised; Antonio in the sequel combines Feliche's role with his own, and so rapidly developes the conception of the Malcontent. He is himself at court in disguise, both the injured prince and the secret courtier awaiting an opportunity for revenge and the exposure of evil.

The Induction furthermore describes Piero as the type of proud duke, who 'strokes up the hair, and struts', as Marston vividly puts it; Alberto the distressed lover; Balurdo the rich fool; Forobosco the parasite and flatterer; Matzagente the braggadoccio; and Castilio Balthazar the affected courtier. In these characters, avowedly typical, we see the immediate effect of the school of humours upon English drama.

The foolish amorist had much attention paid him in the satires, and here he is exemplified by no less than three figures, Castilio, Alberto and coarse Balurdo, all drawn out by Feliche. Thus in a scene which brings one out of melodrama into reality, the foolish little Castilio boasts that he 'cannot sleep for kisses, cannot rest for ladies' letters, that importune him'. Feliche answers sensibly that though he himself has good parts and has attempted courting, he never found the ladies so wondrously 'forthcoming'. When Castilio to prove his case pretends to read from an example of his love-letters: "From her that is devoted to thee, in most private sweets of love, Rosaline", Feliche snatches the letter, and discovers it to be, "Item, for straight canvas, thirteen pence half-penny", something like Falstaff's.[8]

[7] So far as appears in this part.

[8] III, ii, 25f. Castilio Balthazar has much in common with Jonson's Fastidius Brisk, and with the Castilio of Marston's satires. The satire is like that of *Every Man Out*, Feliche taking the part of Macilente. See Baskerville, p. 196, n.

The poor and melancholy lover Alberto speaks (II, i, 135; V, i, 55) couplets echoed from *As You Like It* (III, ii); he ends with a naive withdrawal from the play:

> "For woods, trees, sea or rocky Apennine,
> Is not so ruthless as my Rossaline.
> Farewell, dear friends, expect no more of me:
> Here ends my part in this love's comedy."

The FASHIONS of the time receive comparatively little comment. There is some attempt to keep an Italian background to the play; this and its highly romantic atmosphere both tend to lessen this element of satire. Cosmetics[9] and tobacco[10] are mentioned with disapprobation several times. Beards and tobacco taking are connected twice[11] in this play, as they are often by Marston.

Chief among the CLASSES satirized are rulers and courtiers, the former for their pride and unrighteous government, the latter for their flattery, pride and vanity.[12] The common people he finds utterly fickle.[13] Marston had not really begun his attacks on woman.[14]

In spite of the fact that *Antonio and Mellida* is full of parallels to other plays,[15] thus showing Marston's early interest in the theatre, there is little literary satire. The most important is the parody on the *Spanish Tragedy*.[16] In the Induction the braggadoccio Matzagente begins:

"By the bright honour of a Milanoise,
And the resplendent fulgor of this steel . . ."

when Feliche interrupts: "Rampum scrampum, mount tufty Tamburlaine! What rattling thunderclap breaks from his lips?", indicating the contemporary attitude toward Marlowe's play. Euphuism is also ridiculed.[17]

[9] III, ii, 129f; for rouging see also II, i, 251. For foreign vices, Ind. 102f.
[10] I, i, 126; III, ii, 281.
[11] V, i, 141f. and III, ii, 74. *A. M.* was written probably late in 1599, and shows the influence of *Much Ado* and *As You Like It*, both new plays. Here Rossaline is Marston's coarsened but still wholesome version of Beatrice.
[12] Ind. 7f.; I, i, 76f; III, ii; IV, i, 43f.
[13] IV, i, 70f.
[14] Ind. 87; IV, i, 214.
[15] These references to Shakespeare may be noted: I, i, 247: *Rich. II*, I, iv, 5 (*Globe ed.*); III, i, 1-3: *J. C.* II, i; 73: *Rich. III*, V, iv, 2; 90: *Rich. III*, V, iii, 175; 102: *Rich. III*, V, iii, 277; III, ii, 48: *Sonnet LXVI;* IV. i, 79; *J. C.* I, ii, 228 *(1st Fol.);* V, i, 62: *A. Y. L. I.* III, ii, 93; V, i, 141f.: *M. A. A. N.* II, i, 30. Most of these are not close; Marston generally is not imitative of details.
[16] See Appendix D.
[17] V, i, 228.

The satire of this play, while abundant, is light, as befits
a romantic comedy. Moreover, it is emphatically a humour
play, and as such treats of the minor forms of vice, tending
more towards those of foolishness. So we get attacks on
pride and flattery instead of assaults upon lust. Otherwise,
the satire takes much the same trend as in the *Scourge of
Villainy*.

ANTONIO'S REVENGE [18]

This sequel to *Antonio and Mellida,* as its name indicates,
is a play quite different from that satiric tragi-comedy.
Antonio and Mellida burlesques in one passage an addition
of Jonson to the *Spanish Tragedy,* and draws some lines from
Seneca; [19] aside from these and some echoes of other drama,
Marston depended on himself for the play, so far as is known.
Antonio's Revenge, on the other hand, is a frank working
over of Kyd's plays of the *Spanish Tragedy* and *Hamlet;* it
follows them closely in feeling, incident, and even details. I
have noted some score of similarities to *Hamlet,* and some
dozen to the *Spanish Tragedy.* [20] Seneca is used to a much
greater extent than in the first play; his influence appears in
at least a dozen passages. In this part Marston's attention

[18] Written 1599.
[19] See Cunliffe, Influence of Seneca on Eliz. Trag.
[20] I, ii, 314f: *Hamlet,* II, ii, 528f., also *Sp. Trag.;* II, ii, stage direction: *H.* II, ii, 168, s. d.; II, ii, 56; *H.* II, ii, 575f; II, ii, 139f:
H. III, iv, 9f.; III, i, 32f.: Ghost, at midnight prob. from old *Hamlet;*
84: *H.* I, v, 95f.; 95-6: *H.* II, ii, 291, etc.; III, i, 135, s. d.: *H.* III,
iv, 73; 158: *H.* III, iv, 56; 170f.: *H.* III, iv, 105f.; Cry of "Revenge!"
prob. from old *H.;* III, ii, 65, s. d.: Ghosts second appearance to
mother and son prob. from old *H.;* III, ii, 88: *H.* I, v, 85; IV, i,
s. d.: "Antonio in a fools habit": IV, i, 31-2: *H.* II, ii, 256; 52:
H. II, ii, 612, etc.; 67: *H.* I, iii, 63; IV, ii, 76-80: *H.* V, i, 278f.; V,
Dumbshow, 10: *H.* V, i, 211; V, i, 22: *H.* I, iv, 8; V, ii, 92: *H.* I,
ii, 137. Doubtless there are many others. Has *A. R.* been used in
determining elements of Kyd's *Hamlet?*
    I, ii, 305: *Span. Trag.* III, (ix), 740 (*Everyman ed.,* lines num-
bered by acts); 314f: *ST.* II, (v), 395, etc.; II, i, 21: *ST.* IV, (iv),
246; II, ii, 217: *ST.* III, (ii), 223f.; III, i, 59: *ST.* II, (v), 358, and
III, (xiiA), 915; IV, i, 198: *ST.* III, (vi), 478, etc.; 248: *ST.* III,
(xi), 749-50; IV, ii, 23, s. d.: *ST.* IV, (iv), 344, s. d.; V, i, Dumbshow, ghost-chorus, as in *ST.;* V, i, Dumbshow, 19-21: *ST.* III,
(vii), 508f.; V, ii, 53-4: *ST.* I, 90-1, and last lines of play; 62; s. d.:
ST. IV, (iv), 463, s. d.; 82f.: *ST.* III, (xiii), 1139f.

was focused on the atmosphere and the plot of revenge. Therefore, as would be expected, much less satire is to be found in it; indeed, it is one of the least satiric of all Marston's plays.

Feliche, who was the mouthpiece of most of the satire of the first part, is killed in the second scene. His place as author's representative is partly taken by Antonio, who thus becomes a somewhat more real character than the Antonio of the first part. Occasionally Feliche's father, Pandulpho, speaks for the author. When Antonio is advised to pretend to be a "spitting critic, whose mouth voids nothing but genteel and unvulgar rheum of censure", he answers, "Why, then I should put on the very flesh of solid folly." This ridicule of satire is new for Marston, and may indicate that just at this time he was uncertain as to its value.

There are only a few examples of the abundant MORAL satire found in the first part.[21] Moreover, Marston has abandoned the idea of the HUMOUR play. The humour characters of the first part all reappear in name, but they are practically shorn of their humours, and are kept inconspicuous.[22] For example, Castilio appears often, but does not speak a single word; moreover, he acts far out of his original character as an effeminate courtier. He even aids the duke in strangling Strotzo. In the matter of CLASSES, even that continual butt, the courtier, is scarcely attacked.[23] Actors are mentioned with disfavor a couple of times; probably Marston's attention had been turned to them by the production of *Antonio and Mellida*.[24] There is no LITERARY satire.

This play, then, is not satiric, save that the hero, Antonio, approaches more closely to the type of malcontent which was to become Marston's especial method of satirizing.

[21] Flattery, II, i, 124f.; parasitism, IV, i, 244; vanity, I, ii, 47f.

[22] Except Balurdo, who furnishes most of the comedy, as the sometimes witty, sometimes stupid clown. Forobosco in only one line keeps his character of parasite and flatterer, I, ii, 223f. Matzagente scarcely speaks.

[23] II, i, 117.

[24] II, ii, 109, and I, ii, 315 (where Bullen's *aspish* should read *apish*).

The original Histriomastix was fundamentally satirical. It had been written to oppose the new luxury, and showed a state progressing from Peace, through the stages of Wealth, Pride, Envy, War and Poverty, back to Peace again. It did not seem to contain any personal satire, which Marston added in his additions to the figures of Chrisoganus and Posthaste, discussed elsewhere.[26] This, with a little other LITERARY satire, is all the satiric material which can be credited to Marston.

We find here, I think, one of the last of the attacks of the "University Wits" upon non-university playwrights. The long soliloquy of Chrisoganus[27] which was derived from a speech of Macilente,[28] is made a part of the general assertion of the necessity of university training. Marston speaks for himself through Chrisoganus when the latter exclaims:

> "O, I could curse
> This idiot world . . .
> That crusheth down the sprouting stems of Art . . .
> Crowning dull clods of earth with honor's wreath." [29]

JACK DRUM'S ENTERTAINMENT [30]

This play, produced about 1600, shows another change of method. *Antonio and Mellida* was a humour play; *Antonio's Revenge* had no humour characters. *Jack Drum* attacks some of the methods of Jonson's humour plays, but at the same time goes back to typical humour characters. As such, these are in their essence satiric; therefore we find an increase of satire in this play.

Planet is the author's representative, keeping before the audience the norm from which their humours drive the other

[25] Revised by Marston about the time of the *Antonio* plays, 1599.
[26] *Cf. supra*, pp. 26f.
[27] III, 189f.
[28] *Every Man Out*, opening of Act I.
[29] Cf. III, 197f.
[30] An example of the careless naming of plays. It was intended to recall the popular phrase, *Jack or John Drum's entertainment*, i. e., hard fare. Jack Drum is Sir Edward Fortune's servant, possessing some wit and more brag, but with no such part in the plot as to justify the title.

characters. Planet has much in common with Feliche, and has even something of Chrisoganus. He stands aloof from the rest of the characters, bringing to light their faults, laughing at them, and helping his friends back to sanity. He regards himself as a satirist and the dispenser of justice.[31] It is Planet who concludes the play by forcing the horned cap upon Brabant Senior, the representative of Jonson's dramatic method.[32]

This play frequently shows how satire is really the prevailing mood with Marston, for it intrudes into speeches where it has no business. For example Pasquil, mad for love, says as part of his demented ravings:

> "Let's whip the Senate, else they will not leave
> To have their justice blasted with abuse
> Of flattering sycophants."[33]

And when Camelia says of her foolish lover Ellis, "He is good because he knows not how to be bad," Marston has her maid remark philosophically, "I know not; methinks, not to be bad, is good enough in these days." *In these days* has the true satiric ring.

Satire concerning MORALS is comprised in the treatment of Mammon and John fo de King. "Mammon the usurer, with a great nose" (as he is given in the list of characters) is the villain of the play. Probably his characterisation is influenced by that of Shylock,[34] otherwise we might have expected a closer approximation to the puritan usurer which drew such plaints out of Marston in the satires.[35]

John fo de King is really a HUMOUR character. That is, he was continually upon one subject, had only one aim in life. That this prepossession is lust, would not prevent Marston from considering it a humour, as he had already done in the satires.[36] In John we have an example of how Marston's humour characters are often more individualized and real than Jonson's. Aside from his unquenchable lust, John's figure is

---

[31] IV, 293.
[32] *Supra*, p. 35.
[33] IV, 200.
[34] Simpson, *School of Shakespeare*, I, 208.
[35] *Supra*, p. 101.
[36] *Supra*, p. 103.

not altogether without attractive traits; it seems fitting that his simple, jolly character, evil though it is, should have been the unwitting means of catching the lofty Brabant Senior in his own trap.

The numerous other humour characters show delight in gulling, optimism, fickleness, infatuation, etc.

When we begin to examine Marston's treatment of CLASSES we note a new development — there is scarcely an unfavorable reference to any in authority; even courtiers are only slurred once, out of habit as it were.[37] On the other hand the populace is thus treated: Sir Edward, asked for news of court, answers that it is a

> "Reprobate fashion, when each ragged clout,
> Each cobbler's spawn, and yeasty, boozing bench,
> Reeks in the face of sacred majesty
> His stinking breath of censure! Out upon 't! . . .
> The council chamber is the Phoenix nest
> Who wastes itself, to give us peace and rest."[38]

This attitude is explained by the references to the company which was acting the play, the Children of Paul's. About 1590 both the boys' companies, the Children of the Chapel and the Children of Paul's, seem to have been dissolved. In 1597 there was an attempt made to re-establish the Children of the Chapel, but they did not have their regular theatre in Blackfriars till 1600. However, they may well have gotten the start of the Children of Paul's, whose first recorded play is this *Jack Drum's Entertainment;* certainly they obtained Elizabeth's favour, and it was for a share in this that the Paul's Children were struggling. After having been suppressed ten years, their plays at first seem to have been out of fashion, with an archaic suggestion about them.[39] Marston wrote *Jack Drum* for them in order to refute this charge.

[37] I, 5.

[38] I, 21, 48.

[39] For example, it is known that they produced in this season *The Maid's Metamorphosis,* a Lylian pastoral, *Wisdom of Dr. Doddipoll,* and *Histriomastix.* It was evidently some of these old-fashioned plays which had preceded *Jack Drum.*

136

"SIR ED. I saw the Children of Paul's last night,
And troth they pleased me pretty, pretty well:
The apes in time will do it handsomely.
PLANET. I' faith, I like the audience that frequenteth there,
With much applause; a man shall not be choked
With the stench of garlic, nor be pasted
To the barmie jacket of a beer-brewer.
BRA. JR. 'Tis a good, gentle audience, and I hope the boys
Will come one day into the Court of requests.
BRA. SR. Aye, and they had good plays, but they produce
Such musty fopperies of antiquity." [40]

This is an open bid for court favor, and the play evidently
marks a change in the policy of the management of the Children of Paul's. This activity of the children's companies was
what led to the quarrel with the adult companies, which in
turn permitted, probably fostered, a stage display of the quarrels of playwrights.

On the whole, *Jack Drum's Entertainment* contains little
satire, since it was written solely to amuse, promote the
interests of the Children of Paul's, and especially to win the
favor of the upper classes and if possible the queen. In such
a play satire would have been out of place.

WHAT YOU WILL [41]

Here for the first time since the Satires Marston's pessimism
is fully exposed. Notwithstanding that it is written in a
careless,[42] lively and jocular manner, many parts of it are
singularly unpleasant even for a play of Marston,[43] and for
the first time in his plays there are long passages devoted to
misanthropy. The play begins with the subversive doctrine
that "all that exists takes value from opinion",[44] and Marston's
opinion is that things are pretty bad. Some lines later he
states that "Pity and Piety are long since dead", and Fortune

[40] V, 102f. Cf. Introd.
[41] Written 1601, just about the time of *Poetaster*. Title taken from
that of *Twelfth Night, or What You Will.*
[42] Cf. the artless fashion of I, i, 200; II, i, 265-6; II, ii, 235; III,
iii, 139; V, i, 375: "So ends our slight-writ play".
[43] *E. g.*, III, ii.
[44] I, i, 19; cf. *A. R.* IV, i, 30; *Hamlet*, II, ii, 256.

is not blind, else how could she so unerringly "starve rich worth and glut iniquity"?[45]

Quadratus, who makes these statements, is the author's representative in this play, and is a curious mixture of stoicism and epicureanism. Most characters put forward as the author's own mouthpiece are made likeable, that his statements may have credence; but Quadratus only pleases in that he is somewhat less of a fool than his companions. As his name signifies, he is intended to be the Senecan "four-square" man, and he possesses the stoic philosophy in its bitterest form, but nullified by a simultaneous hedonism. In this same first scene he goes on, excited by the mention of love, to rail at life:

> "Hang love! . . .
> Hate all things; hate the world, thyself, all men . . .
> All things are error, dirt and nothing;
> Or pant with want, or gorged to loathing.
> Love only hate, affect no higher
> Than praise of Heaven, wine, a fire.
> Suck up thy days in silent breath,
> When their snuff's out, come Signior Death."

So he advises the hatred of honor, virtue, riches, beauty, knowledge; all uttered with a grin, to be sure, but at the same time he seems to live up fairly well to what he says. He defies the "sour-browed Zoilist" or critic, and rhymes in what he calls no gleaned poetry, but his known fashion:

> "Music, tobacco[46], sack, and sleep,
> The tide of sorrow backward keep . . .
> While quickest sense doth freshly last,
> Clip time about, hug pleasure fast."[47]

There is more satire of MORALS than in previous plays. A very formal example is the exposure of the condition of London pages.[48] Here Marston seems to have been attacking a very real abuse of the time.[49]

[45] Cf. IV, i, 65f.
[46] Marston's only complimentary reference to tobacco.
[47] II, i, 272. Cf. Quadratus at the end of the play.
[48] III, iii.
[49] For satire on flattery, see II, ii, 220f.; on money, II, i, 305.

The list of characters alone would show that *What You Will* is not a HUMOUR play, as was *Jack Drum's Entertainment*. The only characters who could be considered in this light are the foolish lover Jacomo, a type Marston could never let alone, but who here only serves to start the plot, and then disappears; and the satellite Simplicius Faber. He is evidently a satire on one of the early 'sons of Ben', a foolish 'burr on the nap of greatness'. The youth is nought but admiration and applause for Lampatho:

> "Doth he but speak, — 'O tones of heaven itself!'
> Doth he once write, — 'O Jesu admirable!'
> Cries out Simplicius. Then Lampatho spits,
> And says, 'Faith, 'tis good.' " [50]

Marston is especially apt in such vivid characterizations as this last touch.

Under FASHIONS, Marston has much to say about dress. There is an interesting stage-direction and ensuing scene of foppishness at the beginning of the second act: "One knocks; Laverdure draws the curtains, sitting on his bed, apparelling himself, his trunk of apparel standing by him." Later Marston says "Apparel's grown a god." [51]

Among CLASSES, the ordinary Elizabethan gallant is well described by his page[52]: he eats much and slovenly; he depends on gambling for his money, and only when he has none is his page allowed to carry his purse. "He cheats well, swears better, but swaggers in a wanton's chamber admirably; . . . as contemptuous as Lucifer, as arrogant as ignorance can make him, as libidinous as Priapus." [53]

Albano, a kind of Enoch Arden, abuses woman in an elaborate well-constructed satire in III, ii; it consists of two contrasts between the ideal theory of marriage and the actual practice.

In this slightly written play, designed for the especial purpose of attacking *Cynthia's Revels*, Marston seems to relax his interest in dramatic effect, and slides back into his naturally

---

[50] II, i, 46.

[51] III, i, 11 and ff. The same thought in V, i, 20-41. Beards, save red ones, are envied: III, i. 26; III, ii, 127; IV, i. 31; V, i, 240.

[52] III, iii, 43f.

[53] Other satire on classes III, ii, 18; teachers. II, ii; clergy II, ii, 195.

satiric mood. This is evident from the nature of Quadratus, which approximates to Marston's mood; and it appears in the very wording. "Apparel's grown a god"; love's "grown a figment": here we can discern the usual satiric feeling that the world is degenerating. A new development enters with this play: the world is so evil that the wise man despises it, but with the result that he snatches at the alleviations of pleasure, and decides that "Naught's known but by exterior sense".[54] Here is evidence that the satirist is abandoning his earlier hopes of bettering the world, together with any ascetic ideals he may have had, and now berates simply because it is his accustomed manner of speaking.

THE DUTCH COURTEZAN [55]

In this play some of the changes evident in *What You Will* have proceeded further; humour characters diminish in number and importance, and the proportion of satire increases. Here are brought out Marston's dominant traits; the play treats of lust in the most realistic way; furthermore, the author never surpassed in vividness and reality the varied characters of Franceschina, Crispenella and Cocledemoy. Marston uses for almost the first time contrasted characters; and in certain instances contrives to show character alteration: The loose Freevil and the strict Malheureux of the beginning of the play change places as it progresses; we have the conventional heroine Beatrice[56] and her more lively and free-spoken sister Crispinella, opposed to the world, the flesh and the devil incarnate in Franceschina. In construction the play is the best that Marston had done. The main plot is simple, and derives most of its interest from character-study; it has a steady progression to a climax in the decision of Freevil, and an effective dénouement. The sub-plot, on the other hand, is one of incidents, but they steadily increase in importance. The principal constructive fault is the almost complete separation of the main and sub-plots, though they both end in eleventh-

[54] II, i, 279.
[55] Written late in 1602.
[56] Redeemed into reality by one of Marston's most effective speeches, IV, iv, 63f.

140

hour escapes from hanging. A renewed interest in drama instead of dramatized satire may be indicated in the Prologue:

"The only end
Of our now study is, not to offend.
Yet think not but, like others, rail we could:
Best art presents not what it can, but should."

It is hard to believe that Marston was ever troubled by accusations of not being able to rail.[57]

The author expresses himself somewhat through Freevil[58] and Crispenella. In their speeches they quote, without very much alteration, considerable passages from Montaigne,[59] and his influence is discernible in Marston's new puzzled interest in Nature, by which he means something like natural inclination. Thus Freevil, thinking of the chastity of Malheureux, says that the worst fool is he that would seem wise against Nature,[60] and Malheureux later expresses nearly the same thing:

"Sure Nature against virtue cross doth fall,
Or virtue's self is oft unnatural."[61]

This new thought finds fullest application in Marston's MORAL satire against his favorite adversary, lust, to which the scope of the play gives wide allowance. The *Fabulae Argumentum* is "The difference betwixt the love of a courtezan and a wife." In the first scene Malheureux talks very virtuously, while Freevil half seriously defends lust; the next scene well shows, in the necessarily shortened form of a drama, the rise of passion in Malheureux:

"O, that to love should be or shame, or sin! . . .
No love's without some lust, no life without some love."

[57] Cf. like passages in *Malcontent, infra,* p. 147.

[58] As when he strikes the old satiric note: "What old times held as crimes, are now but fashions", III, i, 284.

[59] Sainmont, *Influence de Montaigne sur Marston et Webster,* Louvain, 1914. He cites the ff. parallels: *D. C.* I, i, 126f: *Mont.* (Florio) III, v, 130; II, i, 66-84: *M.* III, v, 128-9; II, i, 91-2, 98-9, 108-11, 120-145, all from *M.* III, v, 130 and 96-100; III, i, 4-47: *M.* III, v; III, i, 83-5; *M.* II, xii; V, i, 33-7; *M.* III, v; V. ii, 69, 81-90; *M.* II, xii, xxxv.

[60] I, ii, 172. (In Bullen mistakenly numbered 272).

[61] II, i, 84.

Toward the end of the play Freevil expresses again the wonder

> "That things of beauty, created for sweet use,
> Soft comfort, as the very music of life,
> Custom should make so unutterably hellish . . .
>   How vile
> To love a creature made of blood and hell." [62]

In spite of Marston's doubts concerning the reality of virtue, the ultimate aim of the play is to deter from vice; but his methods are more than questionable. The general conception of the play shows a standard of morality which is never quite forgotten, and which the play as a whole is made to serve, thus showing that it is not really decadent. Franceschina is one of the wickedest little persons in Elizabethan drama. She is perfectly alive, and no abstract type; though her evil is made clear, and few readers could wish to know too much of her, yet the sudden passion of Malheureux is quite understandable. It is in details and diction that the play is bad. It has more than the coarseness of the age; it is lecherous and filthy. This is criticism that must be applied to all of Marston's work, and more especially to that which contains the most satire. There can be no doubt that Marston was powerfully attracted by vice — Franceschina must have been drawn from the life; and there can be no doubt that he was even more powerfully repelled. His satire is not hypocrisy, yet it never succeeds in being quite whole-hearted. He dallies too long with vice, and protests too much when he is punishing it. Indeed, he is like the figure he imagines somewhere, of the beadle who itches to possess the whore he is whipping. In this respect, of being the battle-ground of contending passions, he is a characteristic dramatist of his age; he is the antithesis of such a man as Sterne, who was neither good nor bad, but sentimentally suggestive. Marston was both good and bad, and his writings, like Swift's, show the conflict.

The play contains a considerable amount of scattered satire. [63]

[62] V, i, 64f.
[63] For humours, cf. V, ii, 22: under manners: III, i, 7f.; III, i, 64. For classes: III, iii, 10; see also II, ii, 35; III, i, 139, for citizens. Courtiers: IV, iii, 3; V, iii, 149. Poets and parsons: III, ii, 38. Sleeping constables (after Dogberry) : IV, v, 65. Puritans: III, iii. 55; 170. Women: II, ii, 212; V, i, 16; V, ii, 137. Husbands: III, i, 73; IV, i, 30.

To a modern reader this is the most interesting of Marston's plays, in spite of its obvious faults. This is principally because of the play's characterization, and because Marston subordinated satire to drama. What he has to say is expressed through the actions of the characters, and not through shrill words. He was, that is, a satiric dramatist in this play, instead of being, as was more usual, a dramatic satirist.

THE MALCONTENT[64]

The next two plays, the Malcontent and the Fawn, both contain a very large amount of satire, which it will be necessary to give only in summary.

A deeply melancholy vein runs through the high romance of Elizabethan times; and sometimes to this romantic melancholy satire is added. World-famous literary examples of this mixture are Hamlet, and later Byron; it is to this type that Marston belongs. It was especially prevalent in his day, and was not mere affectation, though so this *Weltschmerz* is often regarded. Shakespeare found "the melancholy Jaques" in the society around him; it is this same quality that permeates Hamlet, while Timon is an exaggeration of the type. In real life Montaigne and later Sir Thomas Browne are examples. They both lived soberly in real retirement; Marston while still a young man deserted the reputation he had made for himself, and lived the rest of his life in a country parish. It

The satire of *The Malcontent* shows that it was not written in 1600, as Stoll (*John Webster*, 1905, pp. 55-60) on insufficient grounds has endeavoured to prove. Wallace is more nearly right when he names the spring of 1603, for the *Malcontent's* satire is similar in amount and kind to that in the *Fawn* and *Dutch Courtezan*, both usually dated c. 1604. Wallace (*Children of the Chapel*, p. 101, etc.) dates the earlier plays of Marston: *Hist.*, 1598; *A. M.*, first half 1599; *A. R.*, Nov. 1599; *J. D. E.*, May, 1600; *W. Y. W.*, April, 1601; *D. C.*, fall-winter, 1602; *Malcontent*, spring, 1603. His early dating of *D. C.* places *Mal.* between that and the *Fawn*, which agrees with the satiric elements of these plays: and I have in this paper followed his order.

Wallace states that these dates are for the most part definitely proved, though his evidence is not yet published. In that case, it throws out of consideration the bases for Stoll's conclusions concerning the relations of Feliche, the Malcontent, Jaques and Hamlet, in his paper *Shakespeare, Marston and the Malcontent Type, Mod. Philol.*, Jan. 1906. Cf. supra, p. 77, n., 78, n.

was not 'maukish affectation' which made him be buried "under the stone which hath written on it *Oblivioni Sacrum*". So Byron's Manfred, another example of the same type, demands from destiny

> "Oblivion, self-oblivion —
> Can ye not wring from out the hidden realms
> Ye offer so profusely, what I ask?"

This melancholy of the age was frequently described by the common Elizabethan word malcontent.[65]   It might be called the humour of discontent.   The duke's description of Malevole, near the beginning of the *Malecontent,* sums up the type:

"This Malevole is one of the most prodigious affections that ever conversed with nature: a man, or rather a monster; more discontent than Lucifer when he was thrust out of the presence. His appetite is unsatiable as the grave; as far from any content as from heaven. His highest delight is to procure others' vexation, and therein he thinks he truly serves heaven: for 'tis his position, whosoever in this earth can be contented is a slave and damned; therefore does he afflict all in that to which they are most affected. The elements struggle within him; his own soul is at variance with herself; his speech is halter-worthy at all hours . . .   See, he comes. Now you shall hear the extremity of a malcontent; he is as free as air; he blows over every man."

It is obvious how much this is in accord with the characters of Quadratus and Feliche, though here, as befitted a deposed prince, the character is more bitter. The hero of *Antonio and Mellida* was Marston's first approximation to this type, and his last was in the *Fawn.*   Shakespeare began from the comic rather than tragic side, with Jaques.   *Hamlet* can by no means be properly understood without a knowledge of the Malcontent type; and in *Measure for Measure,* Shakespeare's most Marstonian play, it is interesting to compare the duke with Hercules in the *Fawn.*

[65] Later it came to have a political significance. Nashe's *Pierce Penniless,* 1592, was an early portrayal of this type. Cf. *Gull's Hornbook,* Dekker, 1609 (*Huth Lib.,* ed. Grosart, II, 223): "As for thy stockings and shoes, so wear them, that all men may point at thee, and make thee famous by that glorious name of a malcontent." Cf. Hall's analysis of the malcontent in his *Characters,* 1608. The word was most commonly spelled *male-content.*

The stage malcontent represented a real trait in Elizabethan character. The current stoic philosophy considered malcontentism pathological, as it did love and humours. The textbook of malcontentism is Burton's *Anatomy of Melancholy,* which attempts analysis at great length. It was a symptom of the age, a mentally infectious state which certainly governed Marston himself.[66] This in part explains the tone of his satire. No doubt this tone was partly conventional; but when the convention was added to Marston's temperament, the result was, in Alden's words[67]: "To say that Marston's attitude is pessimistic is to put the facts mildly."

The malcontent type is in essence a humour, partly melancholy, partly cynical, with its natural expression in satire. Marston noticed it in the satires, but did not realize its attraction for him. He savagely attacked exactly what was to be the hero of several of his plays. A man seems to be truly humble and courteous, serving obsequiously without apparent hope of reward:

"O, is not this a courteous minded man?
No, fool, no; a damned Machiavellian;
Holds candle to the devil for a while,
That he the better may the world beguile,
That's fed with shows. He hopes, though some repine,
When sun is set, the lesser stars will shine;
He is within a haughty malcontent,
Though he do use such humble blandishment."[68]

When the malcontent became the principal character in a play, a motive had to be provided to explain his frame of mind, and this was done by making him a high-born, noble character temporarily soured by misfortune. To enable him to utter his satire freely and effectively, disguise was almost inevitable — and here we have the outlines of the protagonist of the *Antonio* plays, of the *Malcontent,* and the *Fawn.*

It is to be noted that satire can best be expressed in drama in a comedy, otherwise the combination of satiric and tragic elements is too heavy. This is true even in Hamlet; in the

---

[66] Prof. Croll suggests that it arose, in Marston at least, from the blending of libertinism (or skepticism) with stoicism.
[67] *Formal Satire,* p. 135.
[68] S. ii, 87-106.

145

acting versions much of the satiric element included in the text is invariably omitted. It is for this reason that the *Malcontent* ends as a comedy, as do all of Marston's plays of this type save *Antonio's Revenge*, where the comparative absence of satire is noticeable. Thus in spite of the obvious fitness of the malcontent for a tragic role, he almost invariably plays a comic one.

There is a steady development of the malcontent character in Marston's plays, until in Malevole, in the play of the *Malcontent*, two originally dissimilar elements have become fused. These are, first, the character in the play representing the author himself, standing aside from the action, but expressing Marston's sentiments and with whom Marston sympathises; second, the romantic, melancholy unfortunate who is the protagonist. Chrisoganus contains the undeveloped germs of both types. In *Antonio and Mellida* we find them clearly divided, in the parts of Feliche and Antonio. In *Antonio's Revenge*, Pandulpho partly takes Feliche's place, but to some extent Antonio unites the types. This play is in a sense a preliminary study for the Malcontent. Planet in *Jack Drum*, though he takes a part in the plot, is clearly of the first type, the author's representative, and so is Quadratus in *What You Will*. Important as Quadratus is in the play, he does nothing; his name does not appear in Bullen's summary of the plot. Albano is something of the malcontent, though he is deceived, instead of playing the customary malcontent role of the deceiver. In the *Dutch Courtezan* Freevil generally expresses the author, having many resemblances to Planet.

Malevole plays the part of both Antonio and Feliche; he is the cynic satirist who most nearly of the characters expresses the author's true opinion, and has the author's sympathy; at the same time he is the disguised exile, who deceives the tyrant and who is the hero of the play. This condensation of interest in one character naturally weakens our interest in other virtuous characters, such as the shadowy Celso, but it permits the presence of two villains as counterweights.

Like other representatives of the author, Malevole has no relations with women in the story: Maria, his wife, has merely a conventional role. Freevil indeed is the only character of this type who is shown in love, and so far as he is,

146

Marston seems to externalize him, treating him as a figure in a play, not as an expression of himself.

Finally, in the *Fawn,* the malcontent character is worn out, and appears for the last time.

The *Malcontent* contains a considerable amount of GENERAL satire, which the preface *To the Reader* shows to have been expected of Marston. Again, Webster in his *Induction* to the play, has Sly insist that it is to be a bitter play. He is answered that it is neither satire nor moral, but history; but that it does not protest to ladies that their painting makes them angels. In the play itself the world is called a prison whose fee for freedom is a man's life. *Stultorum plena sunt omnia,* and the fools go in satin.[69]

The MORAL satire of the play covers practically the entire ground treated in the satires, and again lust is most prominent. Very few of the characters even pretend to morality. In such a world the Machiavellian only goes to the logical extreme.[70] There is more satire on religion than usual, especially on the puritans. Malevole in an outburst against the "deformed church", perhaps lets us catch a glimpse of why Marston was to take orders:

"I mean to turn pure Rochelle Protestant churchman, I . . . Because I'll live lazily, rail upon authority, deny the king's supremacy in things indifferent, and be a pope in mine own parish . . . I have seen oxen plough up altars; *et nunc seges ubi Sion fuit* . . . I ha' seen a sumptuous steeple turned to a stinking privy; more beastly, the sacredest place made a dog's kennel; nay, most inhuman, the stone coffins of long-dead Christians burst up, and made hogs' troughs: *hic finis Priami."* [71]

[69] For general satire, see: *To the Reader; Induction,* 56; I, iii, 57; II, ii, 80; III, i, 65; ii, 76; IV, ii, 25; V, ii, 42; 141; *Ode.* IV, ii, 141 is a typical passage of Malevole: "Think this: this earth is the only grave and Golgotha wherein all things that live must rot; 'tis but the draught wherein the heavenly bodies discharge their corruption; the very muckhill whereon the sublunary orbs cast their excrements: man is the slime of this dungpit, and princes are the governors of these men."

[70] II, i, Mendoza's soliloquy; III, i, 313; IV, i, 233; V, ii, 268.

[71] II, iii, 185f. Cf. esp. IV, i, 180, for evident reality of feeling unusual in Marston; and I, i, 50. Churchmen: I, i, 179; IV, i, 225; IV, ii, 125.

Among CLASSES, princes' favorites and courtiers come in for much attention.[72] Marston was no believer in divine right,[73] but he held the common people to be even more despicable than the aristocracy.[74] Woman as a class has her full share of abuse, principally for being foolish and blind, harming both the good and bad.[75] There are a number of foreign vices mentioned, and an especially interesting passage which seems to refer to the Scotch incursion at court under James I, perhaps even to James himself: *"Bianca:* And is not Signior St. Andrew a gallant fellow now? *Maquerelle:* By my maidenhood, la, honor and he agree together as well as a satin suit and woolen stockings."* Mr. Bullen notes that some copies of the first edition read "St. Andrew Jaques"; the inference from St. Andrew, Scotland's patron saint, and Jaques, the French form of James, is unmistakeable, especially as the daring reference only appears in a few copies.[76]

The lack of HUMOUR characters indicate a late date for the play. Among the references to FASHIONS there is a *Sartor Resartus* idea of equality: All men's souls "are as free as emperors, all of one piece; there goes but a pair of shears betwixt an emperor and the son of a bagpiper; only the dying, pressing, glossing, makes the difference."[77]

The *Malcontent* is perhaps the most characteristic of all Marston's plays. It is satiric in conception, and crammed with details of pure satire. It shows all of Marston's unpleasantness, and exhibits also much that makes his work remembered, just at it ranges over the whole of his satiric field. But in it he does not forget that he is writing a drama; the dramatic and satiric are still fairly well balanced.

[72] I, i, 289; 325; II, iii, 205; III, i, 181f.; IV, i, 52; V, ii, 141. Courtier is named Castilio, I, i, 302.
[73] V, iii, 190.
[74] Mob: III, i, 217; V, iii, 189. Citizens: I, iii, 27; III, i, 61; 107; V, ii, 69; iii, 144.
[75] I, ii, 36; 85; II, ii, 41; iii, 48; 83; III, i, 124; ii, 37; V, ii, 133.
[76] V, iii, 24. Foreign vices: I, iii, 24; III, i, 96; V, ii, 1. Conventional satire of lawyers: I, iii, 49; V, ii, 12; iii, 108. Repeated joke on city official: III, i, 256, V, ii, 212. Poverty of poets, tenants and players: III, i, 259; 37; IV, ii, 4. Money: V, i, 54; ii, 183.
[77] IV, ii, 147; Dress: III, i, 58; V, iii, 13. Cosmetics: Ind., 70; II, iii, 29; III, i, 143. Complication of dances, IV, i, 73. Tobacco: Ind. 136, and note, Bullen; I, iii, 28. Legs and beard: I, iii, 28; V, iii, 36.

PARASITASTER, OR THE FAWN [78]

This play is written in the same vein as the *Malcontent,* and in many ways is a companion-piece. Both are thoroughly satiric. The chief character, the Fawn, is essentially a malcontent, and has the same traits as Malevole, though without the latter's extreme depression. His specialty is to lead foolish men on to make fools of themselves to the top of their bent; then he expatiates to them on their folly, being an adept at 'rubbing it in'. Thus, he encourages the jealousy of Zuccone, and inflames him against his calumniated wife; then, when the truth is revealed, he tells Zuccone to go hang himself.[79] The disheartened Zuccone retorts:

"Fawn, thou art a scurvy, bitter knave, and dost flout Dons to their faces: 'twas thou flattered'st me to this, and now thou laugh'st at me, dost? Though indeed I had a certain proclivity, — but thou madest me more resolute: dost grin and gern? . . . O, I am an ass, true . .

More pity, comfort, and more help we have
In foes professed, than in a flattering knave." [80]

In this interesting passage we see Marston coming to the end of his use for the Malcontent type. It had begun in two distinct types, that of the critical satiric friend, and that of the melancholy unfortunate. These combined in Malevole, who is in the main repeated in the Fawn. But by this time the character had grown too bitter to be regarded in the light of hero. In its exposure of folly it much resembles the gull-baiters of the Jonsonian humour-comedies; and Marston himself had earlier satirized these in the person of Brabant Senior in *Jack Drum.* Between the two unpleasant persons, our sympathies are forced to go to the side of Zuccone, though he had erred so much. For Marston, in endeavoring to show the Fawn a parasite not for his own advantage, but simply

[78] Published twice in 1606; probably produced 1605. The suffix -*aster* of the word Parasitaster was probably suggested by Jonson's title *Poetaster;* but Jonson's suffix had the modern meaning of little, or inferior: Marston's title means that his character had a surface resemblance to a parasite. *Fawn,* in the sense of one who fawns, seems to have been original with Marston; *N. E. D.* gives it as a word used only once, citing however not Marston but a passage dated 1635.
[79] As in *A. M.,* V, i, 55
[80] IV, i.

149

to expose to others their faults, has made him lead them into error farther than they would have gone, and so be himself partly responsible. Moreover, the Fawn does this not from weakness or passion, but deliberately and in cold blood, which still more forfeits our sympathy. Zuccone in the play is made to live and suffer; Marston himself must have felt that the character which he had started to draw as simply a fool had turned into a wronged man. He makes the victim answer in just reproach the Fawn, whose supposed place in the play was to be that of revealing justice, or nemesis. With this natural development, the malcontent character is really used up. Marston himself begins to half-dislike him, and we are not surprized when the type does not reappear in the plays, in spite of the fact that it was Marston's most characteristic contribution to the drama. His satiric spirit had again, in another direction, overleaped its mark.

In the prologue', Epilogue and Address to the Reader, Marston shows that he was intending to write a SATIRE. Its scope is that of Juvenal's satires, he says; he quotes Persius; he defies detraction, in all three. The odd satiric flavor of Marston is shown at the end of the Prologue, where after much praise of his audience he shows he has been ironical, by ending:

> "Now that if any wonder why he's [the author] drawn
> To such base soothings, know his play's — *The Fawn.*"

This turning upon his own work and half-satirizing it, half-satirizing the audience, is characteristic of Marston; it gives the whole an air of insincerity, when he meant only irony.

Here he speaks of "my bosom friend, good Epictetus", and traces of Stoic philosophy are as numerous as in the Malcontent. It is easy to see how this vein of thinking would tend toward satire, though in its origin so opposite. The malcontent is a preacher of stoicism, engaged in *demonstrating* how unstable is good-fortune, how uncertain the future, how weak man's endeavors; as examples he uses the lives of those around him. So the Fawn begins with the stoic (and Christian) doctrine, "He that doth strive to please the world's a fool;" because, he goes on to say, chance is more powerful than knowledge or virtue. In that case the world is a bad place. When the idea of degeneracy is added, the present is an iron age descended from the former golden age; and the stoic has turned typical satirist. The philosophy which began by decrying passion has changed until it swells with satiric wrath, the least stoic of passions.[81]

In the satire of MORALS, flattery would be expected to be most important, emphasised as it is by the title. The disguised middle-aged duke wins favor by continual flattery, the "grateful poison, sleek mischief, dreamful slumber, that doth fall on kings as soft and soon as their first holy oil."[82] But nevertheless lust, as usual, has the most important place, notwithstanding a surprising passage in the Prologue decrying:

> "that most common sin
> Of vulgar pens, rank bawdry, that smells
> Even through your masques, *usque ad nauseam.*"[83]

There are no true HUMOUR characters in this play, at least in the original sense — characters who are continually referring to one petty thing which in reality is not a real part of their nature, but can be sloughed off. Here we tend to return to the simple type play, where characters have only one side, and any rounding of individuality is not attempted. Thus, the old Duke Gonzago is the senile type, with one especial trait, belief in his own diplomacy; doubtless he is drawn from Polonius. Bullen[84] is with cause inclined to suspect that in this character Marston was glancing at the 'wise fool' King James; at any rate, there is similar satire in the *Malcontent* and *Eastward Ho.*

Throughout Marston's literary work he displays scorn of foolish lovers; in this play the satire culminates, with a cluster

[81] Cf. such passages as I, i, 56; I, ii, 350; II, i, 21; 33; V, i, 23.

[82] I, ii, 329; 334; II, i, 50f.; 592; beginning of III, i.

[83] Apparently this passage prompted Wm. Sheares, who published Marston's plays, 1633, to say that the author "is free from all obscene speeches; . . he abhors such writers, and their works." Langbaine read the play, but quotes this statement with approbation, and holds Marston up to admiration. Langbaine had wide influence on early uncritical writers on the drama, as in early biographical dictionaries and dramatic cyclopedias and prefaces. It is curious that such a legend should have started in regard to Marston of all dramatists.

For references to lust, see I, ii, 70f.; IV, i, 2f.; Aphrodisiacs: II, i, 150; 581; V, i, 365.

[84] Vol. I, p. xliii.

of types. Nymphadoro loves every lady extremely well, and is not inconstant, he says, to anyone in particular.[85] Herod Frappatore is the boaster.[86] Zuccone is the needlessly but desperately jealous husband.[87] Sir Amoroso Debile-Dosso is an older Nymphadoro. All this satire on foolish love is summed up in the last act, in a Masque of Cupid, when all foolish offenders against love are consigned to the Ship of Fools.

Under CLASSES may be included general satire on woman; and Marston's harshest railing against woman is here in abundance. "Women are the most giddy motions under heaven. . . Only mere chanceful appetite sways them".

"Why did not heaven make us a nobler creature than woman, to sue unto? . . . But that we must court, sonnet, flatter, bribe, kneel, sue to so feeble and imperfect, inconstant, idle, vain, hollow bubble as woman is! Oh, my Fawn!"[88]

Marston had written thus, though not at so great length, again and again; but here there is a difference. The above quotation is spoken by jealous Zuccone, half mad at believing himself cuckolded. His mistake revealed, the Fawn in derision repeats some of these his words to him, to emphasize his errors. Moreover, in the play there is another new feature, several passages in praise of woman.[89]

There are a considerable number of references to LITERA-TURE, of which the most important are those to the *Ship of Fools*. The idea of Barclay's 1509 translation of Brandt's

[85] I, ii, 52; III, i.

[86] After recounting his exploits, he sighs, "Fie on this satiety! — 'tis a dull, blunt, weary and drowsy passion." IV, i, 100f. This is directly from Florio's Montaigne, II, xv, which is again copied in Webster's *White Devil*, II, i. Cf. *I Henry IV*, II, iv, 117.

[87] Characterized II, i, 205.

[88] IV, i, 401f. Similarly, I, i, 62; II, i, 92; III, i, 470; IV, i, 118.

[89] III, i, 521; IV, i, 568; 598f. The only approach to this had been some of the contrasts between wife and prostitute, in *D. C.*, and between the flighty and constant sisters in *J. D. E.*, (IV, 301.)

For other satire, see (courtiers) I, ii, 22; II, i, 82; IV, i, 182; 208; 289. (Foreign vices) II, i, 106; 330; IV, i, 61; 333. (Informers) I, ii, 255. (Politicians), IV, i, 202; (Priests) IV, i, 210. (Philosophers), IV, i, 235. (Drink) V, i, 168; cf. *D. C.* I, i, 106. (Tobacco) IV, i. 5; V, i, 361. (Beards and legs) I, ii, 90; 297; V, i, 320.

Narrenschiff furnished a kind of rallying point for Marston's satire in this play — the collection of all kinds of folly for exile. The Ship of Fools is mentioned by name no less than eleven times in the play,[90] while V, i is devoted to a court in which classes of foolish lovers are successively sentenced to the ship. Marston borrowed little or nothing from this book except the name.

He attempts to give the impression that his inspiration was classical, by quoting the satirists Martial, Persius and Juvenal, the last twice.[91] He calls Epictetus his bosom friend,[92] though there is less open stoic philosophising than in the *Malcontent*. But Marston owes much more to Florio's Montaigne, which he does not mention — almost a hundred lines, philosophical or sententious.[93]

As in most of Marston's plays, it is easy to find Shakespeare's influence. Gonzago seems to be copied from Polonius. Hamlet's satire on old men is partly repeated by the Fawn[94]; Marston's favorite passage in *Richard III* is again parodied.[95]

In this play are to be found clear indications of another quarrel with playwrights.[96]

In this play the satire definitely overbalances the drama. Marston's satire here passes the indifferent, stoic stage, and becomes a positive thing of evil, watering the roots of folly and crime in order that the fruits may be the more abhorrent. — until the plot is submerged in a black sea of suspicion and misanthropy.

[90] I, ii, 33; III, i, 139; IV, i, 89; 192f.; 560; V, i, 47; 245; 285; 310; 384, 401; 437.

[91] *Equal Reader;* opposite Act I.

[92] *Equal Reader.* Cicero mentioned, IV, i, 633; cf. 689.

[93] Sainmont, *Influence de Montaigne sur Marston et Webster: Montaigne,* III, v: *Fawn,* III,, i, 212-3; 221-37; 251-2; 270-3; IV, i, 112-16; 119-40; 359-74; 377-81; 385-89; 392-3; 396-400; 587-91; V, i, 20. *M.* II, iii: *F.* III, i, 214-18. *M.* II, xii: *F.* IV, i, 237-41. *M.* II, xv: *F.* III, i, 243-4; IV, i, 107-8.

[94] V, i, 80. Given in Bullen to Herod, a mistake for *Herc.,* i. e. the Fawn. *Hamlet,* II, ii, 198. These similarities help to date the *Fawn* after Hamlet.

[95] V, i, 43. Bullen notes II, i, 212 is from *Rich. III.*

[96] *Cf. supra,* p. 78.

In this play, the work of Chapman, Marston and Jonson, the satiric element of Marston's share alone will be traced.[98] Though he wrote two-fifths of the play,[99] there is little satire to be found; evidently his bent was altered by the company in which he worked. This influence must have been due to Chapman; Jonson's influence would not have diminished the satiric element.

So, under MORALS, the absence of almost any satire on lust is most noticeable.[100]

In this city play, it is natural that there should be considerable comment on CLASSES. It is a bourgeois drama, and no favor is given to 'gentlemen'. The sparking Quicksilver says that though he is an apprentice he can give arms. "I am a gentleman, and may swear by my pedigree. . . Do nothing, be like a gentleman, be idle." [101] Marston was writing this only four years after Jonson had ridiculed his gentility in the *Poetaster*.

Marston's famous satire against the Scots is the best-known fact concerning the play. According to the French ambassador's gossip, players had gone scandalous lengths in representing and ridiculing James I, showing the new alien monarch as drunk and cursing.[102] His Scotch thrift in putting up knighthood for sale aroused contemptuous indignation, which is expressed in a passage in the first quarto of *Eastward Ho*, wishing the Scots out of England into Virginia.[103] Later Chapman wrote from prison that the chief offences were but two clauses; the other seems to be the passage where Sir Petronal Flash asks aid of two gentlemen, one of whom says of him: "I ken the man weel; hee's one of my thirty pound

[97] Composed probably less than a year before its entry in S. R., Sept. 4, 1605.

[98] See Appendix F for division.

[99] 2979 lines in Bullen's ed. of play; Marston wrote about 1154.

[100] V, v, 188; this, compared to the similar passage in the *Fawn*, shows the end of the play is by Marston.
The treatment of Quicksilver and his 'punk' is scarcely satiric.

[101] I, i, 194f; cf. IV, ii, 220f.

[102] Thorndike, *Shakespeare's Theatre*, p. 216. Day's *Isle of Gulls* in the same year may have satirized royalty (Fleay, *Chr. of Eng. Dra.*, I, 108-9.)

[103] III, iii, 42-50; the only passage omitted in later quartos.

knights," the player presumably imitating James' well-known accents.[104]   Years later Ben Jonson in a famous passage told to Drummond of Hawthornden the result of these indiscretions:

> "He was delated by Sir James Murray to the King, for writing something against the Scots, in a play *Eastward Hoe,* and voluntarily imprisoned himself with Chapman and Marston, who had written it amongst them. The report was, that they should then had their ears cut, and their noses. After their delivery, he banqueted all his friends; there was Camden, Selden, and others; at the midst of the feast his old mother drank to him, and shew him a paper which she had (if the sentence had taken execution) to have mixed in the prison among his drink, which was full of lustie strong poison, and that she was no churle, she told, she minded first to have drunk of it herself."

Three undated letters of Chapman and four of Jonson have been preserved, to the King, the Lord Chamberlain, the Earl of Salisbury, etc., imploring the authors' release. No mention is made of Marston, and some modern authorities assume that he was not imprisoned.[105] But in Antony Nixon's *The Black Year,* 1606, Marston is referred to as

> "bringing in the *Dutch Courtezan* to corrupt English conditions, and sent away westward [i. e., imprisoned] for carping both at court, city and country. For they [satirists] are so sudden witted that a flea can no sooner frisk forth but they must needs comment on her."

It has been argued that the letters refer to another joint imprisonment of Jonson and Marston, but this is improbable.[106] The solution may be that Marston, the youngest of the three, aged 28, an Oxford graduate and married to the daughter of the King's Chaplain, was of higher rank than his associates, and was consequently soon released; we know that the prisoners were dealt with individually from one of Chapman's letters to the Lord Chamberlain. This would explain the fact that Marston's name was not mentioned in the poets' letters, were they written subsequent to his release.

[104] IV, i. This presumably would have been the passage to arouse Murray's wrath, but it was not deleted; possibly the English censor, while against any slight to the king himself, did not object to injured Scotch feelings, otherwise.

[105] Schelling, *Eliz. Drama,* I, 507; Thorndike, *Shak. Theatre,* 217.

[106] Schelling, introd. to *Belles Lettres* ed. of *Eastward Ho.*

Whatever LITERARY satire there is, comes from Quicksilver's penchant for quoting tags from plays.[107]   The reading
of romances is satirized in Gertrude, and Marston contrives
to turn this into satire on contemporary knighthood. When
her husband has taken her money and run away, Gertrude
complains:

"Would the Knight o' the Sun, or Palmerin of England, have used
their ladies so, Sin? or Sir Launcelot? or Sir Tristram? . . . They
were knights of the Round Table at Winchester, that sought adven-
tures: but these, of the square table at ordinaries, that sit at hazard." [108]

It is a few such passages as this, with their emphasis on
now-a-days, that show the old satirist was still present, though
restrained by collaboration.

THE WONDER OF WOMEN: OR SOPHONISBA

Sophonisba, produced about 1606,[109] seems to have been the
last play written entirely by Marston. It contains comparatively little satire, though it starts out in the old fashion with
attacks on "reputation, thou awe of fools and great men", and
on envy. MORALS are scarcely mentioned, unless it be in the
portrayal of Syphax's lust.[110]

What satire there is, is upon CLASSES, and principally
woman. The very title shows Marston's apparent surprise

[107] As Bullen notes, this is probably derived from Shakespeare's Pistol. Quicksilver quotes the *Spanish Tragedy* thrice: I, i, 129; II, i,
118; 138f. *Hiren,* II, i, 115; *Tamburlaine,* II, i, 91; *Rich. III,* III, iv, v.
"Via the curtain that shadowed Borgia", II, iii, 25, is referred by Bullen
to Mason's *Muleasses the Turk,* but the parallel is far from close, and
Mason's play does not date earlier than 1607 (Schelling, I, 447.)
[108] V, i, 35.
[109] In Preface to the Reader, *Fawn,* 2nd Qto., 1606: "I will present a
tragedy to you"; Bullen notes: " *'Sophonisba'.*— Marginal note in the
second Qto." He does not state whether printed or written, but presumably the former, else he would have been more explicit. Without
this note the 'tragedy' might have referred to *Insatiate Countess.*
Schelling (*Eliz. Drama,* II, 26-7) dates *Soph.* 1603, because of its
preface slurring *Sejanus,* played 1603. But this preface, with its "relating things as a historian", and "transcribe authors, quote authorities",
obviously relates to the publication of *Sejanus* in 1605.
[110] There are one or two general satiric lines, such as II, i, 172; iii,
102.

that a woman could be constant and virtuous. This astonishment at the phenomenon of a fine woman was expressed in several other plays, notably in the *Fawn*,[111] where there is what might be an advance sketch of *Sophonisba*:

> "A prodigy! let Nature run cross-legged, . .
> Cold Saturn crack with heat, for now the world
> Hath seen a woman!" [112]

The satirist shows what he thought of women in general by putting abuse of her sex into the mouth of the shining exception. Sophonisba speaks of the "low appetite of my sex' weakness", and repeats, among other things, what Crispinella had said in the *Dutch Courtezan*, that women have to pretend to be modest.[113]

In several passages the crowd is satirized;[114] and the Machiavellianism of princes is set forth at some length.[115]

The only LITERARY satire is the reference to *Sejanus*.[116]

This lustful melodrama shows a breaking down of Marston's powers for satire as well as for drama. His obscurity of style is increasing, and as he before had observed in the case of Hall, obscurity is fatal for satiric effect. The play is seemingly written simply to startle, and contains little merit of any kind.

THE INSATIATE COUNTESS

This was a late play of Marston's, perhaps his last. Probably it was left unfinished by him, and was completed by Barksted.[117] Barksted's reworking of the play was so thorough that it seems impossible to separate Marston's share, save from the style of passages here and there. There is little satire in the play save on lust and woman; but much of this seems in Marston's vein. The Countess herself is a

[111] *Fawn*, IV, i, 598.
[112] *Soph.* II, i, 156.
[113] I, ii, 20. See also I, i, 75; I, ii, 177; 184; II, i, 138.
[114] Prologue; II, i, 130; II, ii, 17.
[115] II, i, 55.
[116] *Cf. supra*, p. 78.
[117] About 1610-13; he probably added all the subplot and revised what Marston had done. See Small, *Harvard Studies in Phil. and Lit.*, V, 227.

157

Dutch Courtezan transplanted to high life; and is in addition a nymphomaniac. Marston may have intended Mizaldus to be the author's representative, but he soon drops out of the play as we now have it. There are a number of passages on woman which sound Marstonian, such as "Man were on earth an angel but for woman. . . . Women are made of blood, without souls;" someone "has compiled an ungodly volume of satires against women, and calls his book *The Snarl*."[118] The following sounds Marstonian in its conciseness:

"He turns religious upon his wife's turning courtezan. This is just like some of our gallant prodigals,—when they have consumed their patrimonies wrongfully, they turn Capuchins for devotion."[119]

There are a few uncomplimentary references to foreigners.[120] Finally we have the familiar mentions of small leg and red beard.[121]

SUMMARY

Eleven plays have been attributed to Marston; of these he wrote eight alone, two tragedies and six comedies, while he revised or collaborated in a kind of morality play, *Histriomastix;* a comedy, *Eastward Ho;* and a tragedy, the *Insatiate Countess.* His two tragedies, *Antonio's Revenge* and *Sophonisba,* show little satire; the same is true of the plays of joint authorship.

His six comedies, then, contain his dramatic satire. The writing of these plays extended over only six or seven years, but in that time it is possible to observe a definite development of their satire, considered apart from any personal quarrels.

Antonio and Mellida is not much more than a long satire on pride and flattery, provided with a highly romantic plot. It is clearly by a satirist trying his hand at drama, and with rather more regard for the satire than the play. Helped by its romance, *Antonio and Mellida* seems to have proved a.

[118] I, i, 58; II, iii, 96; III, iii, 36; III, iv, 175f., IV, ii, 86; 106; iii, 38; iv, 47; V, i, 87.
[119] I, iv, 60.
[120] I, i, 470; III, i, 135; IV, i, 27.
[121] I, i, 224; II, ii, 37.

success. When Marston wrote its sequel, *Antonio's Revenge*, he was clearly under the fascination of his new attempt at the dramatic form, and satire temporarily was neglected for a thrilling play of revenge. In these two plays appear the elements of his main satiric type, the malcontent.

Jack Drum's Entertainment was a carelessly composed humour comedy, written for the purpose of puffing the Children of Paul's. Satire glances through it, here and there, but. as tragedy is too heavy in itself to make a good vehicle for bitter satire, so light comedy is too gay-hearted to carry it in any bulk. The next play, *What You Will*, is even more carelessly written as a play, and we find Marston continually slipping away from his business as a dramatist to his old occupation of satirist. Quadratus in this play carries to a height Marston's favorite device of making a certain character the author's mouthpiece. This is essentially a device for escaping from the demand of drama,—that the author's thought be given to the audience primarily in the form of action. The loose, oratorical style of much of Elizabethan drama made easy such a misuse as Marston employed in these representatives of his, who commonly have little part in the plot.

Another development of this play is the increased misanthropy of the satire. Previously Marston had possessed the younger, more hopeful mood where satire is administered to reform vice. Now it sours into something very close to hatred for the world as a whole. He certainly despises mankind. Moreover, he begins to doubt the validity of moral laws. He seeks a refuge for his discontent in opposite directions, in enjoyment of the fleeting moment. and in stoic egotism and impassive self-containment. He seeks both because neither alone satisfies his character compounded both of strong passion and an eager intellectual force which disdains passion. One mark of this increasing bitterness is his attack on woman, which begins in this play. Previously he has merely alluded to them as incidental factors in man's degeneracy. From now on he assails them as foolish creatures strong in nothing but libidinous desires. None of his women essay to be wise, and virtue in them is either a miracle or the result of lack of opportunity.

159

The Dutch Courtezan personifies this new hatred for woman. With a definite object of attack instead of mere disdain for society in general, he regains the power of writing strong drama. To make his realistic picture of the pretty, deadly Franceschina effective, he contrasts with her a woman of normal virtue, one of the very few in his work who are not mere puppets. Thus he makes stronger both drama and satire.

The *Malcontent* brings to a height in the title-role the principal satiric type which Marston developed. This development necessarily progressed as it did. To be effective the protagonist must have some elements of nobility. If he is to rail at the world and disclose its follies and vices, he must have been deeply injured; if he is to rail in safety, he must be disguised. Hence the dispossessed ruler in disguise at his own court. Moreover, here Marston can combine into one satiric figure the mouth-piece of his own snarling philosophy, and the hero of the plot, before, separate figures. This character is then draped in the melancholic gloom which was familiar to the age, and the result is the best possible figure to utter satire dramatically.

In his next play, the *Fawn*, Marston attempts to repeat this character, and does express a vast amount of satire; but his malcontent type-figure is alive enough to refuse to stay at the fullness of his power; he decays, through exaggeration, and loses the modicum of nobility which Malevole had possessed. Since he does not have our sympathy, his utterances lose their effect. Malevole managed to retain for himself the belief of the audience that he represented the norm of truth and right conduct from which the other characters of the play departed; the Fawn on the other hand is a member of the ignoble crowd, only slightly cleverer than the mass of knaves and fools which surround him; he loses, that is, any moral authority in the drama.

Moreover, the satire under which the play staggers is lower in quality than previously. His treatment of lust is more disgusting, and yet weaker; here occurs his harshest railing against woman, but it is stultified by being for the most part uttered against one of his ladies of miraculous virtue; his vituperations against flattery and hypocrisy are uttered in a more strident voice, but are not for that the more effective.

Marston's last important play was a failure, both as drama and satire.

For a little the influence of his dramatic superiors, Jonson and Chapman, lifted him up to the point where he could write intelligently and well, in his share of *Eastward Ho*. A year later he attempted to repeat the early success of *Antonio's Revenge* by writing *Sophonisba*, an ultra-romantic melodrama, this time motivated by crude lust. Before he withdrew from the stage in disgust, he seems to have attempted (possibly under the influence of Chapman's *Byron*) a revival in high life of an historic Dutch Courtezan, but either he never completed it, or it was of such quality that it alone of his plays had to be worked into shape by another man.

Marston's satire began in wrangling, and ended in failure. In all probability he would never have been a great writer; his genius had too many faults for that. But it is interesting to speculate what might have been his measure of success had he lived in an age when novels instead of poetic dramas were the literary fashion. He could never submit himself for any length of time to the rigid restrictions of dramaturgy; he was next to nothing as a poet. Had his gifts for satire, depiction of real life, and vivid characterization been employed in the looser form of the novel, it is possible that his name would bulk much larger than it does in literary history.

APPENDIX A

I — REFERENCES TO HALL IN THE SATIRES

Auth. in Praise ll. 35-40. Grosart asserts (p. 35) Mastigophorus is Hall. Elsewhere he says the name must be general for satirist. The passage calls Mastigophoros an epigrammatist, however; he is not Hall.

S. ii, 14-36. Marston has said he wrote amorous poetry, so was not immaculate (a confession Pygmalion was not a satire). Then he says modern satire is so obscure no one can understand it, without the help of a mythological dictionary and Delphic Apollo. On the lines

> "Who could imagine that such squint-eyed sight
> Could strike the world's deformities so right?"

Grosart has an odd note: "Query. Was Hall squint-eyed?" He might have made this an assertion had he also noted SV. IX, 25. Of course the passages referred to Hall's style, though he at least twice declares that he writes too plainly (*Lib. III, Prol;* beginning of *Biting Satires.*) But Marston is clearly right in his criticism—cf. Hall, *Lib.* II, i; IV, i, for obscurities. In his *Postscript* he says IV. i was intentionally vague, the rest clear; but they are not.

S. iv. Reactio. All written directly against Hall, because of the way he detracts from others. *Lines 5-8* are a short preliminary parody of Hall's *Defiance to Envy*. *Lines 9-32* are a satire on satire, which could be applied to Marston as well as to Hall. The name Grillus comes from the *Faerie Queene* (II.xii, 87) through Hall (II, ii, 66). *Lines 33-108* defend poetry against the attacks of Hall. Each of the sacred poems attacked in *Virg.* I, viii are praised: Robert Southwell's *St. Peter's Complaint,* 1595, and, *The Virgin Mary to Christ on the Cross.* (Cf. Southwell's *Mary Magdalen's Funeral Tears,* 1591; Markham's *Mary Magdalen's Lamentations for the Loss of her Master Jesus,* 1601.) The "sacred sonnets" are Markham's *Poem of Poems, or Sion's Muse,* containing the *Divine Song of Solomon in Eight Eclogues,*

1595. Hall later, doubtless converted by Marston, made some poor versifications of the Psalms. Next Marston defends translation, which *Virg.* had not attacked, and defends the *Mirror for Magistrates,* which Hall had parodied (V, i). Then Marston says:

> "What, shall not Rosamund or Gaveston
> Ope their sweet lips without detraction?"

Daniel had written a *Complaint of Rosamund;* Drayton, a *Legend of Pierce Gaveston,* but they are not mentioned by Hall, altho Alden (p. 142) attempts to connect the latter with Hall's satire on the *Mirror for Magistrates,* because of distant similarities. Marston seems to have used these two poems simply as examples of the romantic poetry which he thought Hall attacked in I, v. *Lines 109-130* defend adventurers (probably both had Raleigh's expedition of 1596-6 in mind) as extravagantly as Hall had condemned them (*Virg.* IV, iii, 28; III, i, 54; IV, vi, 36). *Lines 101-2* on the "prudent pedant" Bullen refers to Hall, who had interrupted his Cambridge course by teaching. *Lines 130-154, 163-6,* are a parody on Hall's *Defiance to Envy* (quoted with references supra, p. 14). At the end, *167-70,* he advises Hall to cease satirizing poetry, and to laugh with him at "strangers' follies."

SV. In Lec., 77. "Some spruce pedant. . . striving to vilify my dark reproofs." Hall had been called pedant (SV. IV, 102); Marston may be referring to the verses pasted in *Pyg.*

SV. III, 111f. In this obscure passage Hall is the "academic starved satirist" who "would gnaw reezed bacon." (Cf. *Virg.* IV, ii, 36, attacked SV. III, 165). The meaning seems to be that Hall lashed trivial crimes, while greater ones were unpunished. He asks (l. 160) if the world is to be left infected, while Hall attacks spendthrift Villius, because he keeps a man, a hood, and silver handled fan, with only forty pounds a year. These words are taken from *Virg.* V, iv. Hall (IV, ii) ridiculed a farmer who starves himself to send to the university a son who is ashamed of the father, learns law, and finally climbs into a good marriage and wealth. So Marston writes (l. 165), in contempt of Hall's poverty at Cambridge (Athens):

163

"Or snarl at Lollius' son
That with industrious pains hath harder won
His true-got worship and his gentry's name
Than any swineherd's brat that lousy came
To luskish Athens and, with farming pots,
Compiling beds, and scouring greasy spots,
By chance (when he can, like taught parrot, cry
'Dearly beloved', with simpering gravity)
Hath got the farm of some gelt vicary,
And now, on cockhorse, gallops jollily;
Tickling, with some stol'n stuff, his senseless cure,
Belching lewd terms 'gainst all sound literature."

Marston goes on (l. 177) to ask if he too, like Hall, shall fight against shadows, trivial things; or "task bitterly Rome's filth", which both Marston and Hall did (*Virg.* IV, iii). Rome here, however, might possibly stand for London.

Proemium in Lib. II. Marston says in a passage referring to Hall, "I cannot quote a mott Italianate or brand my satires with some Spanish term." Cf. *Virg.* V, ii, 47 and its ridicule of Maevio "with his big title and Italian mot," which Grosart suggests refers to Lodge's *Fig for Momus.* This has an Italian motto on its title-page, but the title is not "big". Hall had before the first satire of his second volume an Italian motto, and Marston is probably turning Hall's own words back on himself. Hall mentions Spanish subjects frequently (I, iii, 29; III, vii, 27; IV, i, 27; iv, 45; V, iii, 48) but never justifies Marston's line.

SV. VI, 36. An author does not dare publish till he has tremblingly invoked Colin Clout. Cf. *Virg., Defiance to Envy,* l. 107; stanzas 9 and 10 are devoted to Spenser.

SV. IX, 21-37. The lines preceding this refer to another critic of poetry, whose suit is satin and who is bearded. Hall is the "Athens' ape," i.e., the Cambridge plagiarist; he patches an oration and squints at good poetry, unthankful for its merits. This ill-tutored pedant beslimes "Mortimer's numbers," probably Drayton's *Mortimeriados,* 1596, though *Virg.* does not refer to Drayton at all. The "spruce Athenian pen" of the lines following is not Hall, but "sage Mutius" who writes in a "tricksy, learned modern vein." The passage is obscure; it seems to be Marston who is praising Mutius in the lines in quotation, 48-53. "Silent" may mean 'not here named by Marston'; "whose silent name one letter bounds,"—

I can only think of *Barnabe Barnes* and *Nicholas Breton* whose names are in a sense bounded by one letter. Both were Oxford men; but Barnes had been harshly dealt with by Marston (cf. supra, p. 111); and "true judicial style" well fits Breton's work. *Lines 54-71* are criticism of yet another author who wrote obscurely, not Hall, since the author links senseless prose with clear poetry (as Sidney's *Arcadia* was written in both prose and verse). This whole passage has been carelessly supposed by Schulze and others to apply to Hall.

SV. X (*Satira Nova* added in ed. of 1599), *27-76.* Marston asks of Ned (Edward Guilpin), who is the gallant who cuckolded his own elder brother, and thereby lost his expected inheritance by getting his brother an heir? Alden suspects Marston meant to infer that he was the older satirist, and that Hall had assumed the name; but the allusion would be little apposite, and Marston would have been clearer if claiming such a point. The "elder brother" may mean poetry, which Hall had satirized, so attacking his own work. Cf. end of *S. iv.* Marston goes on to say, very truly, that he had been too subtle, and addresses Hall more openly (thus proving that the previous paragraph concerned him). Hall, he says, had been praised; this made the "Master's hood" so proud that he wrote "An Epigram which the Author *Virgidemiarum* caused to be pasted to the latter page of every *Pygmalion* that came to the Stationers of Cambridge". Its point seems to be the application of Marston's pseudonym, Kinsayder, to himself. Marston then complains that the world has fallen in love with Hall's satires, while he himself, on a sickbed and soured by the misapplied praise of Hall, scorns the honor of being a poet and says he will write no more. Thus Marston confesses that the antagonist he had apparently wantonly chosen, had triumphed in popular estimation, and that he himself was giving up the struggle in disgust.

II — MARSTON'S BORROWINGS FROM HALL

S. i, 114. *Steaming stew.* As in Virg. IV, i, 132.
S. ii. 16f. Obscurity of satire. Cf. Pro. III, and IV, i.
S, iii, 51f. *Inamorato Lucio.* Cf. I, vii.
    66-70. From IV, ii, 85-9.

SV.   In Lect., 2; and IV. 17.   *Dunghill peasant.*   As in III, i,
78; IV, v, 97.

SV.   *To Detraction.   To Oblivion.*   Cf. Hall's *Ded. to Oblivion, and Prol. Lib. IV*.

SV. I, 15.   *Simpering Lesbia.*   Cf. IV. i, 156.

SV.   III, 75.   *Snout-fair.*   Cf. IV, i, 111.

   68.   *Camphire and lettuce, etc.*   Cf. IV, iv, 109f. and VIII,
56.

   139.   *Streak his limbs.*   Cf. VI, i, 206.

   162, and VIII, 133.   *Silver-handled fan,* etc.   Cf. V, iv,
11-12, 22.

   165.   *Snarl at Lollius' son.*   Cf. IV, ii.

   173.   *Gelded vicaries, etc.*   Cf. IV, ii, 102, 106, etc.

SV. IV 20.   *Botching up balladry.*   Cf. I, i, esp. l. 9.   Prob.
both from classical sources.

   58.   *Aquinian* (i.e., Juvenal).   Cf. IV, i. 2.

SV.   Prol. Lib. II.   Same stanza form as Hall, *Prel. Lib. IV*
and *Pyg*) l.   *Italian mott.* Cf. I, iii, 25; V, ii, 47.

SV.   IX, 34.   *Esculine.*   Cf. IV, i, 58.

There are several other similarities of subjects satirized,
but without evidence of imitation.

APPENDIX B

MARSTON'S SHARE IN *HISTRIOMASTIX*

This play as we have it seems almost such a mixture of features as our comic opera or revue presents today.   This is
largely due to the mutilated and mixed form of the play which
we have.   That it is not a deliberate hodge-podge is shown
by the total difference in style and character-portrayal of the
middle and the two ends of the play.   This was not the result
of simple collaboration, because the play has two endings,
both preserved; first, a logical return to the conditions at
the beginning of the story; second, a court ending roughly
tacked on.   Moreover, there are two plays within the play,
neither as we have it given at its necessary original length;
and there is much confusion among the names of minor characters.

That the adaptor was Marston has been proven (Simpson,
School of Shakespeare, II; Small, *Stage-Quarrel,* 69f.) ; whole

scenes are in his unmistakeable style—forceful, coarse, crabbed lines with a tang all their own. The style of the original play is almost featureless in comparison, save that it is sometimes stilted and academic. Cf., for example, III, 189-209 with I, 84-90. In the main the Marstonian pasages are in a single section and stand out clearly, i.e., III, iv (180) through V, i, (60).

Before this section, however, there are four passages which are Marston's. The first is II, i (63-7), quoted supra, p. 26. Compare the wording with the opening of SV. Proem. in Lib. I :

> "I bear the scourge of just Rhamnusia
> Lashing the lewdness of Britannia."

It seems to be an attack upon Jonson's words in the Induction to *Every Man Out:*

> "I'll strip the ragged follies of the time
> Naked as at their birth — and with a whip of steel
> Print wounding lashes on their iron ribs."

The second Marstonian passage is an interpolation for the sake of attacking Monday, II, ii (126-131) ; Posthaste speaks after giving some extempore verse :

> "I never pleased myself better, it comes off with such suavity.
> GULCH. Well, fellows, I never heard happier stuff,
> Here's no new luxury or blandishment,
> But plenty of old England's mother's words.
> CLOUT. I'st not a pity this fellow's not employed in matters of state?"

This passage contains the only two consecutive lines of blank verse in the non-Marstonian player scenes. "Luxury and blandishment" sounds like Marston, who uses the word *luxury* frequently, while I have noted *blandishment* in S. ii, 104; SV. III, 124; SV. VIII, 90; and Jonson makes Marston-Crispinus use it in his first speech, *Poet.* II, i. Marston uses the introductory *well* much oftener than any other like word in *Histriomastix*, while it is scarce in the non-Marstonian portion.

There is too little evidence to make a decision possible concerning the players' song, II, iv (247-54). It includes the

167

statement that the players singing it are the fourth company in town. In 1596, the date of the old play, there are records of only two men's companies (though there may have been stray performances by others), and no children's companies were performing. In 1599 the two children's companies seem to have been playing, also. But this, though it indicates Marston's authorship, does not prove it. The position of the song does not help, as it follows work of the old play, and is succeeded by a Marstonian portion.

There follows the prologue and interlude of *Troilus and Cressida* II, iv (255-80), by Marston. In the surviving version there are the remains of two interludes here, only one of which is required by the play. The *Troilus and Cressida* one sounds much more like Marston than does the archaic *Prodigal Son*. The lines 260-1 are echoed in the undoubtedly Marstonian IV, 193-7.

The first ten lines of Act III sound more alive and rich than the old play, and can be identified as Marston's by comparison with a speech of Mammon's in *Jack Drum's Entertainment*, III, iii, beginning: "My ship shall kemb the ocean's curled back."

When we approach the end of the bulk of Marston's undoubted work, III, iv through V, i (60), there is much uncertainty. V, ii (the conscription of the players) is left doubtful by Simpson, given to Marston by Small, and to the old play by Hoppe. It has little of the Marstonian style, and resembles in some ways the arrest of the players, VI, v (187), so perhaps it too should be assigned to the old play. It does nobody any credit. V, iii (103) is Marston's at least till the entrance of the mob (147); the concluding speech of Chrisogonus is also obviously Marston's (181-191). The intervening mob scene can be safely given to him also, because of its context and superior force. When we reach V, iv (192) we are safely in the old play again. The evidence is mostly negative, but the absence of Marston's distinctive style is noticeable.

Act VI is almost all the old author's. In scene v Marston may have added some touches to the character of Posthaste, such as line 235: "I'll boldly fall to ballading again." The old play had originally closed with a paean of Peace, as it had begun. Marston inserted before the song, "With Laurel",

(257-8) the stage direction "They begin to sing, and presently cease", and he added the court ending which follows the song. For an evidence of Marston's style, cf. lines 278-9: "the world's Empress, Religion's Guardian, Peace's Patroness", with the *Ded. to Nobody* of *A. M.*: "honor's redeemer, . . . virtue's advancer, religion's shelter, and piety's fosterer."

In summary, Marston wrote II, i, 63-7; ii, 126-131; iv, 247-254 possibly; 255-280; III, i, 1-10; III, iv (180) through V, i (60); V, iii; in VI, v, probably some touches to character of Posthaste; VI, vi, 259-end (295). Thus Marston wrote 487 lines in the middle of the play, and some 168 lines scattered through other portions. Altogether he would have to his credit about 655 lines, a quarter of the play's total of 2601 lines.

APPENDIX C

THE ORIGINAL OF LAMPATHO

Some traits of Lampatho do not fit into our conception of Jonson. He wears satin; he says repeatedly "I protest"; he is a pessimist; he has studied philosophy for "seven springs". The one passage, however, which has misled most critics, is that in II, i in which Quadratus addresses Lampatho with the words, "Why, you Don Kinsayder!" (Passage quoted supra, p. 46-7). Marston had used Kinsayder, or Kinser (dog-gelder) as a pseudonym and play on his own name, before SV., and it was applied to him in the II *Return from Parnassus*, I, ii. Therefore Marston and Lampatho have been identified, by Penniman and several others. (Schelling, *Eliz. Drama*, I, 488, seems from his footnote to follow Penniman, but his statement is somewhat ambiguous: "Marston seems to have retaliated on Jonson with his own hand in the character Quadratus.")

It is certainly odd that Marston should have applied his own pseudonym to the man he was attacking, and if practically all the other evidence were not against it, it would warrant taking Marston as Lampatho's original. As it is, Lampatho is essentially Jonson; the character of Marston seems to afford the only explanation of the contradiction. He was a complex character, and was in the habit of looking at himself as a separate person. Thus he sneers repeatedly at his own poem

Pygmalion, which yet had been written with evident zest; almost every one of his plays contains jests at red hair and little legs, which it seems from the *Poetaster* were characteristics of Marston. This attitude of double personality may explain how he could use his own recognized *nom-de-plume* as a term of abuse for an antagonist. He seems to give it the meaning of 'malicious satirist.'

There are a few other traits of Lampatho which do not fit Jonson, but it must be remembered that no character in any of these plays is identical with the person it satirized.

Penniman endeavors to prove that Quadratus was meant for Jonson, by a number of very weak arguments, such as the fact that a speech of Quadratus (II, i: "No, sir, should discreet Mastigophoros, etc.") imitates a speech of Crites in *Cynthia's Revels,* III, ii. But obviously Marston was turning Jonson's own thunder back upon him. Again, Quadratus says that he beats Lampatho. Jonson claimed to have beaten Marston; but Marston would scarcely have boasted of it in a play. Again, Penniman deduces from the words, "He and I are of two faiths" that Jonson's Romanism was indicated — an idea which a glance at the phrase's context would dissolve. Other minor suppositions of Penniman it is scarcely necessary to disprove.

In this quarrel we have the two most satiric of Elizabethan dramatists satirizing each other because the other *is* satiric. Each uses in his satire much the same terms as does the other. Hence between Quadratus and Lampatho there is not such a vast deal of difference, save for the light in which they are presented. When a strong false scent, like the "Don Kinsayder" passage, is drawn across the true trail, it is not entirely the fault of the critical hounds if they be thrown off the scent.

APPENDIX D

PARODY OF THE *SPANISH TRAGEDY* IN *ANTONIO AND MELLIDA*

This has been the cause of some curious critical misapprehensions. Henslowe paid Jonson £2 on September 25, 1601, for additions to Kyd's *Spanish Tragedy* (called by Henslowe *Geronymo*). He paid £2 more on June 24, 1602, part of which was for additions. These additions were first printed, according to the title-page, in 1602, after being popular on the stage. *Antonio and Mellida*, entered October 24, 1602, printed 1602, contains a comic passage (beginning of Act V) which is parallel in many ways with a passage in Jonson's additions, concerning Hieronimo's distracted request to the painter to paint impossibilities, (end of Act III, scene xiii, or xiiA, *Everyman ed.)*

Penniman and Small, noting that *Antonio and Mellida* was produced as early as 1599 (it was ridiculed in *Every Man Out*, February or March, 1599/1600), state that Jonson must have imitated Marston. All internal evidence points the other way. Jonson's bizarre conception of a speaking picture would lend itself to parody, and the scene Marston wrote would be a natural kind of parody. Again, the wording is enough alike so that audiences would be reminded inevitably of the other play; is it conceivable that Jonson would try to produce effect from material which must remind his audience of pure farce? Moreover, the *Antonio and Mellida* passage has no connection with the rest of the play, and very little meaning in itself unless it be supposed a parody.

It is possible, and under the circumstances almost certain, that in the interval between Jonson's addition, which may have been produced as early as the autumn of 1601, and the publishing of Antonio sometime in 1602, Marston inserted his lines burlesqueing Jonson's passage. Penniman notes this possibility (p. 100) but discards it because he says the "War" was then finished. But *Satiromastix* appeared in the autumn of 1601, and the Apologetical Dialogue even later. The "War" was not definitely at an end before the dedication of the *Malcontent*, 1604, so far as we can tell.

There have been several additional suppositions concerning this passage of *Antonio and Mellida*. It has been supposed to parody *Cynthia's Revels*, the painter being "undoubtedly Jonson"; or, Marston was alluding to Jonson's attacks upon him, since he mentioned his own age, 24. (See Fleay, *Chr.* II, 75; followed by Penniman, *War*, 98, and partially by Small.) These are all without ascertainable bases of fact, and are improbable.

171

APPENDIX E

I — CLASSICAL SOURCES OF SATIRES

A list of allusions and quotations, which in no case are of any special importance. Doubtless many other details of similarity could be discovered, for Marston was well acquainted with his classics; but I have satisfied myself that from no literary source did Marston draw any considerable amount of material for his satires.

Juvenal

S. i, 51. Democritus laughing. Cf. Juv. *Sat.* X, 33.
     124. Can bear with sinners, not hypocrites. Cf. II, 15.
SV. I, Title. Quoted from II, 8.
     5. Adapted from X, 221.
     19. *Glassy Priapus.* From II, 95.
  II, Title. Quoted from I, 30.
     Score of opening lines. Cf. first part of I.
     115. *Son doth fear his stepdame.* From VI, 628.
     118. *To be huge, is to be deadly sick.* Cf. VI, 629.
  III, 90. No lust satiates Messaline. Cf. VI, 130.
     195. *Gloomy Juvenal, though to thy fortunes I disastrous fall.*
  IV, 58. *There is a crew which I too plain could name If so I might without th' Aquinian's blame.*
  V, Motto and subject. Somewhat like I, 73.

Persius

S. i, 124. *Break my spleen with laughter* (occurs several times). Cf. Per. *Sat.* I, 12.
SV. Title-page, motto. Quoted from I, 44. Cf. Juv. XIII, 16; Martial, III, 2.
  VI, 7f. Poetry inflames readers. Cf. I, 20f.
     9. *Glavers with his fawning snout.* From I, 34.

Martial

SV. II, 124. *Silver pisspots.* Cf. Mart. *Epig.* I, 37.
  199. Lesbia shameless. Cf. I, 34.
  III, 151; *Rich Crispus.* Cf. X, 14.
  IV, Title, *Cras.* Cf. V, 58 (but prob. from Persius.)
  V, 95. Poor Irus. From VI, 77.

Ovid

SV. VIII, 72. Soldiers in love. Somewhat like *Amores,* I, 9; *Odes,* I, 10.

Catullus

SV. To Perusers, 37; XI, 178. *Suffenus.* Foolish poet often ridiculed by Catullus.

Cicero

SV. X, Motto. *Stultorum plena sunt omnia.* From ad *Fam.* 9. 22. 4.

Marston makes use of about 90 names of classic origin, of which only 16 had been used by Hall, and only 37 by classical satirists. Four *(Crispus, Laelius, Rufus* and *Tullus)* had been used by Horace, Juvenal and also Martial; *Publius* by Persius instead of Juvenal. Other sources were Tibullus *(Albius);* Terence and Plautus *(Chremes, Gnatho, Saturio);* and Ovid *(Corinna, Julia).* Juvenal gives him 16 not in other sources, Persius only 3. Hall seems to have furnished him with 4, which do not appear in the other usual name-sources *(Furious, Lynceus, Martius, Villius).*

Six names have Italian forms *(Bruto, Brownetta, Castilio, Cornuto, Luxurio, Roscio);* one is Spanish *(Hiadalgo).* He uses only two plain English names *(Harry, Ned).* *Tegeran* and *Tubered* appear to be either invented or anagrammatic names. (SV. III, 95; Pro. Lib. II, ad Rhy., 23.)

There is a partial list of these names in Grosart's edition of Marston's poems.

APPENDIX F

THE AUTHORSHIP OF *EASTWARD HO*

This problem has attracted workers on Jonson and Chapman, but has not before been treated from the standpoint of Marston. The first attempts to assign the respective shares of authorship were made by Dodsley *(Old Plays,* 1744, Vol. IV, Pref. to E. H.) and "J. C." an author in *Blackwoods* (Sept., 1821; X, 136). Others who have attempted partial analyses are Swinburne *(George Chapman,* 1875, pp. 55f.), Bullen *(Works of Marston,* 1887, I, xxxvii), Ward, A. G. *(Hist. Eng. Drama,* 1899, II, 441) and Schelling *(Jonson's E. H. etc., Belles Lettres Series,* xiif). Complete assignments of authorship have been made by Fleay *(Biog. Chron.,* 1891, I, 60-1; II, 81-2) and thoroughly by Cunliffe (Gayley's *Rep. Eng. Comedy,* II, 401-4) and Parrott *(Comedies of Chapman,* 1914, pp. 841-8 and notes). With the two last critics I for the most part agree, save that I venture to assign some parts rather more definitely to Marston than even Parrott has done. There follows evidence on contested scenes.

Cunliffe's comparison of the Prologue to that of *Bussy D'Amboise* is not weighty, as that prologue is improbably

Chapman's from its date; only one of Chapman's comedies has a prologue *(All Fools)* and that in quite a different vein. The Prologue of *Eastward Ho* is Jonson's. It has been agreed that the first act is Marston's.

The middle of II, i is indubitably Marston's; there are play-tags, abundant echoing of phrases, a typical passage (l. 149) which can be paralleled in *Dutch Courtezan*, IV, v, 14; finally the Cocledemoy of that play resembles the drunken Quicksilver.

The short II, ii (Bullen's division; the opening speech of the long second scene in Parrott's ed.) is Marston's because of the artless introduction of Security by himself (cf. Touchstone in I, i); and a phrase from this scene is repeated in II, iii, 24, which is in a Marstonian portion.

II, iii for the most part shows little of Marston, seems too light to be Jonson's, and may be Chapman's. But there are two Marstonian passages; lines 1-60 have such lines as:

> "O witty age! where age is young in wit,
> And all youth's words have greybeards full of it,"

> "And in thy lap, my lovely Dalila,
> I'll lie, and snore out my enfranchised wit."

The rude imitation of a ballad which follows is quite in Marston's vein. The second Marston passage is in lines 198-238. It is Cocledemoy Quicksilver who

> "Hopes to live to see dog's meat made of the old usurer's flesh, dice of his bones, and indentures of his skin; and yet his skin is too thick to make parchment . . . Your only smooth skin to make vellum is your Puritan's skin; they be the smoothest and slickest knaves in the country."

Another reason for believing that Marston and Chapman may have interwoven their work here is that this scene marks the division between Marston's and Chapman's work. As Fleay doubtless observed when making his unexplained division (in the main correct), Eastward Ho scarcely pretends to interweave the main and sub-plots. The main plot engrosses the first three scenes (which Fleay assigned to Marston) and the last six (which he gives to Jonson); the sub-plot is scarcely interrupted during the middle seven scenes (which he gives to

Chapman). The scene in question (II, iii) contains the transition from main to sub-plot.

Bullen noted on III, i, 20, that Marston also used 'wedlock' in the sense of 'wife' in the Fawn; but so do Middleton, and Chapman (All Fools). The scene is Chapman's.

The satire on the Scots in III, iii, 44-60, has always been attributed to Marston on the strength of Jonson's assertion; it is however possible, though not characteristic, that Jonson might have laid the offending passages to Marston's charge after Marston alone had been freed from imprisonment (cf. supra, p. 154). At any rate, the rest of the scene is plainly Chapman's, as attested by the stage-directions "surgit" and "ambo".

The little fourth scene continues the subplot; but its style is different and sounds Marstonian; moreover it ridicules a line of *Richard III* which Marston has parodied frequently elsewhere; I believe it to be by Marston.

The subplot is wound up in IV, i, a scene in the main by Chapman. The mimicking of James I has always been ascribed to Marston, again because of Jonson's statement in his letter of appeal to the King: "Your two most humble and most prostrated subjects . . .: Geo. Chapman and Ben Jhonson, whose chief offences are but two clawses, and both of them not our own." He naturally does not mention Marston's name, even if he were thinking of him; it might be that the passages in queston were mere actors' interpolations. The Scot satire in III, iii is in the middle of a passage drawn from the *Utopia*. This satire was omitted in later editions, but the satire in IV, i remained. It is possible that the "two clawses" referred to the two sentences of the first passage, that were excised. This passage may be Marston's; it is in his satiric spirit. But the attribution is not certain. The scene does contain a passage obviously Jonsonian, swarming with technical terms of alchemy. The end of the scene, with its apostrophe to the horn, is certainly Chapman's.

The main plot is recommenced with IV, ii, and though Marston's style is not very well marked, I believe it to be by him, especially after the entrance of the women and up to about line 264. In this portion there are many echoings of phrases, and Marstonian expressions are used such as "cullion", "marry, first o' your kindness", "hunger drops out at his

175

nose", "gold-ends", and "head fastened under my girdle." At about line 264 the style changes, and may be Jonson's. The last speech is by Marston.

It is agreed that Marston wrote V, i. At line 81 there comes an abrupt change in the current of thought, and possibly the fairy speech, to line 102, is Jonson's.

No one but Jonson could have written the list of denominations (lines 33f.) in V, ii, and the scene is his, as is the rest of the play until near the end. Marston wrote the close of the play, after V, v, 156 and the entrance of the women. The mother and Girtred are his particular property, and there are several other indications, separately slight, such as the mention of "Bow-bell" (used twice before in Marston's part, — Bullen, pp. 15, 19) ; the suddenly frequent use of the introductory "why"; the citizen's cap, etc. The six rhyming lines at the end may be compared to other scene endings of his in I, ii and II, ii.

The Epilogus, like the Prologus, was, I believe, written by Jonson.

ATTRIBUTIONS OF AUTHORSHIP OF EASTWARD HO

Division (Bullen)	Plot	Fleay	Cunliffe	Parrott	Mine
Prologue	....	..	C	J	J
I, i	Main	M	M	M	M
ii	Main	M	M	M	M
II, i	Main	M	C	M	M
ii	Sub	C	C	M (J?)	M
iii	Main				
	Sub	C	C	M, C, M at end	C (M, 1-60, 198-238)
III, i	Sub	C	C	C	C
ii	Main				
	Sub	C	C	C	C
iii	Sub	C	M	C (M, Scots)	C (M, 44-60,?)
iv	Sub	C	..	C or M	M
IV, i	Sub	C	C (M, J)	C (M, J)	C (M?, J)
ii	Main	J	C	M (revised by J)	M (J, c. 264-337)
V, i	Main	J	C	M (revised by J)	M (J, 81-102,?)
ii	Main	J	C	J	J
iii	Main	J	C	J	J
iv	Main	J	C	J	J
v	Main	J	C	J	J (M after 156)
Epilogue	....	..	..	..	J

176

As will be seen, I have for the most part (independently) agreed with Parrott as against Cunliffe. I rather doubt, however, the current ascription of the Scotch satires to Marston, as they are both embedded in the work of Chapman, and Jonson's statement does not mention Marston. I have also assigned the ending of the play to Marston.

BIBLIOGRAPHY

Alden, R. M. *Rise of Formal Satire in England under Classical Influences;* U. of P., Philadelphia, 1899.

Baskerville, C. R. *English Elements in Jonson's Early Comedies;* U. of Texas, 1911.

Boas, F. S. *Works of Thomas Kyd;* Oxford, 1901.

Bullen, A. H. *Works of John Marston;* Houghton, Mifflin; Boston, 1887.

Burton, Robert. *Anatomy of Melancholy.*

Cambridge History of English Literature; Putnam, 1907-11.

Collier, J. P., ed. *Shakespeare* (works), London, 1858.

A Bibliographical and Critical Account of the Rarest Books in the English Language . . . ;Joseph Lilly, London, 1865.

Cunliffe, J. W. *Influence of Seneca on Elizabethan Tragedy;* Stechert, New York, 1907.

Dekker, Thomas. *Plays;* ed. R. H. Shepherd, 1873.

(See Penniman)

Gulls' Hornbook, 1609; Huth Library, ed. Grosart, II, p. 223.

Dictionary of National Biography; Macmillan.

Dodsley, Robert, ed. *Select Collection of Old Plays;* London, 1744.

Fleay, F. G. *A Biographical Chronicle of the English Drama,* 1559-1642; Reeves & Turner, London, 1891.

Chronicle History of the English Stage; Stechert, 1890.

Shakespeare manual; Macmillan, London, 1876.

Chronicle History of the Life and Work of Shakespeare, 1886.

Gayley, C. M., ed. *Representative English Comedy;* Macmillan, 1912-1914.

Gifford, W., ed. *Works of Ben Jonson;* W. Bulmer & Co., London, 1816.

Grosart, A. B., ed. Occasional Issues (privately printed).

Bishop Hall's Complete Poems, 1879.

Marston's Poems; Blackburn, 1879.

Hake, Edward. *News out of Powles;* Isham Reprints, 1872.

Halliwell-Phillips, J. O. *Outlines of the Life of Shakespeare;* 6th ed. Longmans.

Harington, Sir John. *Metamorphosis of Ajax* . . . ; Whittingham, Chiswick, 1814 (reprint).

Hart, H. C., ed. *Works of Ben Jonson;* Methuen, London (1906).

Henslowe, Philip. *Henslowe's Diary,* ed. by W. W. Greg; Buellen, London, 1904.

Hoppe, (Felix) Fritz. *Histriomastix-studien;* Diss. Fleischmann, Breslau, 1906.

Jonson, Ben. (See under Gifford, Hart, Judson, Mallory, Penniman, Schelling.)

Judson, A. C., ed. *Cynthia's Revels;* Yale Studies in English, Holt, 1912.

Kerr, M. *Influence of Ben Jonson on English Comedy;* Appleton, 1912.

Kyd, Thomas. *Spanish Tragedy;* Everyman ed., Minor Elizabethan Drama, v. ii. n. d. Dutton.
(See under Boas)

Lee, Sir Sidney L. *Life of William Shakespeare;* Macmillan, 1899. Revised edition, 1916.

Magnus, Laurie, ed. *Documents Illustrating Elizabethan Poetry, by Sir Philip Sidney, G. Puttenham, and W. Webbe.* Dutton, 1906.

Mallory, H. S., ed. *Poetaster;* Yale Studies, Holt, 1905.

Marston, John. (See under Bullen, Grosart.)

Massey, Gerald. *Secret Drama of Shakespeare's Sonnets Unfolded;* 1872.

Meres, Francis. *Palladis Tamia;* Arber's English Garner, reprint.

Nash, Thomas. *Pierce Penilesse his supplication to the diuell;* ed. J. P. Collier, Busbie, London, 1870 (1592).

Nason, A. H. *Heralds and Heraldry in Ben Jonson's plays;* Nason, New York.

No Whipping nor Snipping . . . (Nicholas Breton) ; Isham Reprints.

Ordish, T. F. *Early London Theatres;* London, 1899.

Parrott, T. M., ed. *Comedies of Chapman.* Dutton, 1914.

Penniman, J. H. *War of the Theatres;* U. of P., 1887.
ed. *Poetaster and Satiromastix;* Belles Lettres Series, Heath, 1913.

Puttenham, George. (See under Magnus). *Art of Poesie.*

Sainmont, J. *Influence de Montaigne sur Marston et Webster;* Louvain, 1914.

Schelling, F. E. *Elizabethan Drama,* Houghton Mifflin, 1908.
ed. *Complete plays of Ben Jonson,* Everyman ed., Dutton, 1910.
ed. *Jonson's etc., Eastward Ho, etc.;* Belles Lettres Series, Heath, 1903.

Schulze, Konrad. *Die Satiren Halls . . . ;* Palaestra cvi; M. J. Müller, Berlin, 1910.

Shakespeare, William. Globe text; Cambridge ed., Houghton, 1914.

Shakespeare's England. ed. Onions, C. T.; Oxford, 1916.

Sidney, Sir Philip. *Defense of Poesie;* ed. A. C. Cook, Ginn.

Simpson, Richard. *School of Shakespeare . . . ;* Boston, New York, 1878.

Small, R. A. *Stage-quarrel between Ben Jonson and the so-called Poetasters;* Forschungen zur Englischen Sprache u. Literatur Pt. 1. Breslau, 1899.
Authorship of Insatiate Countess, Harvard Studies in Philol. and Lit., V, 227.

Stevens, H. *Life of Thomas Harriot;* priv. print., Portland, Me., 1900.

Stoll, E. E. *Shakespeare, Marston and the Malcontent Type;* Mod.
    Phil., Jan. 1906.
    John Webster; Harvard, 1905.
Swinburne, A. C. *George Chapman;* London, 1875.
    Age of Shakespeare, Harpers, 1908.
Thorndike, A. H. *Shakespeare's Theatre;* Macmillan, 1916.
Wallace, C. W. *Children of the Chapel at Blackfriars;* Priv. Printed,
    1908.
Ward, A. W. *History of English Dramatic Literature;* Macmillan,
    1899.
Winchester, C. T. *Some Principles of Literary Criticism;* Macmillan,
    1899.
Winckler, Carl W. *John Marston's litterarische Anfänge;* Diss. Bres-
    lau, 1903.
    Marston's Erstlingswerke u. ihre Beziehung zu Shakespeare;
        Eng. Stud., xxxiii, 1904.
Wood, Anthony à. *Athenae Oxonienses* and *Fasti;* ed. P. Bliss, 1820.
Wyndham, G. *Poems of Shakespeare;* 1898.

INDEX

Most titles, except of dramas, are referred to under author's name only.

181